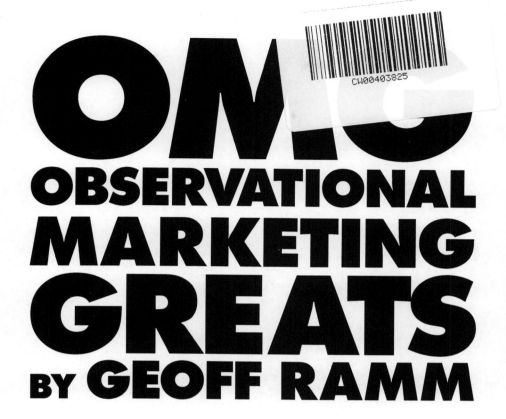

OMG
OBSERVATIONAL
MARKETING
GREATS
BY GEOFF RAMM

First published 2012 by Creative Juice Publishing
www.geofframm.com

ISBN-13: 978-1478344094
© Copyright Geoff Ramm

Book Design: Gabrielle Imerson, Public UK
Copywriter: Liz Hardy, Plays With Words
Helen Stothard, HLS Publishing Solutions

RAVING REVIEWS

"I have read many marketing books, most of them I don't like. But this is one you just have to read".
Nigel Risner, Motivational Speaker & Author

"Geoff's book is spilling over with fabulous examples of observational marketing that provide the reader with masses of 'brain food' for bringing more creativity into their business and personal marketing. Being different is a requirement of success in today's business world and this book truly provides all that is needed to invigorate a creative process to standout from the crowd. If you're serious about your brand being noticed, then you cannot afford to ignore this book!"
Lesley Everett, Personal Branding Speaker & Author

"OMG, this is not like other marketing books. Geoff Ramm encourages his readers to stand out from the crowd and be different and this book achieves exactly that. Crammed full of real life marketing observations that make you laugh, nod and applaud, OMG should inspire you to come up with great new marketing ideas for your own business. Standing out from the crowd has never been easier".
Andy Lopata, Business Networking Strategist and author of '... and Death Came Third!' and 'Recommended'

'Geoff Ramm is not only a marketing genius he shows you how to become one too. Quite possibly one of the easiest and most powerful books you'll ever read on the subject of marketing ever, you'll be laughing as well as learning'
Paul McGee The SUMO Guy, Motivational Speaker & Author

"WHEN THE COMPETITION GOES ONE WAY, DO YOU FOLLOW THEM? OR OD UOY OG EHT REHTO YAW?"

GEOFF RAMM MARKETING SPEAKER

FOREWORD

When you've watched a man fly halfway around the world and step out onto the stage in Tehran, and within 60 minutes hold nearly 1000 Iranians completely in the palm of his hand, it's impressive. When you've seen the same individual be flown back to South Africa for a private one-day session with some 60 odd marketing delegates at a leading South African FMCG company, following a rave review appearance at its Sun City conference ~ you know you've met someone who is clearly not just good at presenting, but really knows their stuff.

Geoff Ramm has 'wowed' audiences everywhere with his consummate grasp of what makes for modern, successful marketing and communications. I have watched him speak myself now on numerous occasions, and like his audience members all across the planet, I've quite simply been enthralled every time. Whether it's his observational marketing style, his stage presence or just the way his brain ticks… Geoff has an innate power to captivate and inspire…

Which is precisely what the content of this book will do for you.

It's a quirky collection of things the man sees, thinks and does, and it should leave you wanting more. For your business, your career and for yourself. So enough of the foreplay; go straight ahead, and dive in...

MICHAEL JACKSON
GLOBAL CHANGE SPEAKER
MICHAEL@THEOTHERMICHAELJACKSON.COM

CONTENTS

"WHEN CREATIVITY MEETS OPPORTUNITY...

GREAT MARKETING HAPPENS"

GEOFF RAMM, MARKETING SPEAKER

AND ALL BECAUSE THE LADY LOVES...

My obsession with all things marketing began when I was just 3 years old.

Thanks to a habit of watching far too much television since 1977, I have a mind full of adverts, slogans, jingles, music and characters from the world of marketing, including my all-time favourites: the Smash robots, the Dulux dog, and the Jolly Green Giant.

At the age of 6, my only ambition in life was to become the next Milk Tray Man. Swooping down the pristine slopes on my skis, box of chocolates secreted away under my jacket; creeping into the bedroom and leaving the Milk Tray box on the bedside table, And All Because The Lady Loves…

I guess sneaking into a room in such a manner probably wouldn't be acceptable these days, but back then it was the dream. With its James Bond looks, this one advert broke the mould of how to market and sell chocolates, and it's the one piece of marketing which has stuck firm in my mind for over 30 years.

So let me start this book with my Milk Tray challenge:

How will you be remembered in 30 days? How will you be remembered in 30 months? How can you stand out so much that you and your business will be remembered in 30 years' time?

To be remembered you need to do something different. When the competition are all going one way, do you follow them? I thought not. You have to stand out from the crowd. Go the other way. Step out of the comfort zone and into the spotlight.

Observational Marketing Greats is crammed full of my most memorable Observational Marketing stories and ideas from businesses – large and small – who have done just that.

I hope you will take some inspiration from how these great businesses stand out from the crowd so that you too can be talked about, for all the right reasons, for years to come.

I've had the pleasure of working with some amazing people and businesses and have had the honour of speaking in some of the most wonderful countries in the world. This book is dedicated to everyone I have met along the way, everyone who has ever been in the audience, but most of all it is dedicated to my two girls and little master Ramm, who are my true inspiration for everything I do.

YOU ARE AN OBSERVATIONAL MARKETEER; YOU JUST DON'T KNOW IT YET...

It's a skill we all have. We're all secretly really good at it, and we're doing it all the time. It's called Observational Marketing.

WARNING! This is NOT theory. It's better than theory: it's real life marketing, and it works! Embrace the Observational Marketeer within and breathe hundreds of new ideas into your business.

How many times will you see a great slogan, a brilliant advert, or experience fantastic service? 99% of the time you will acknowledge it, smile, or even comment, but that's it... you do nothing more about it. Through the course of this book you will sharpen your observational skills to help boost the marketing success within your own business.

In the simplest terms, all you need to do is observe the positive and negative aspects of marketing and RECORD THEM! The promotional signage that stops you in your tracks; the radio advert that made you turn the volume up, not down; the customer service that made you feel all warm inside.

Everything that delights you, surprises you, and leaves you with a smile on your face. But also take note of the bad stuff: the poor signage; the awful customer service; the marketing that shocked and appalled you. Whether you whip out your camera phone, camcorder, or use an old-school pad of paper and a pen, make sure you get those Observational ideas down and you'll rapidly find yourself armed with dozens of new marketing ideas – the great and the not so great.

SO WHAT DO I DO WITH ALL THESE RANDOM IDEAS, GEOFF? — GOOD QUESTION!

Take them along to your next marketing meeting (Tip No. 1: always have a marketing meeting!). Share your ideas and observations with the rest of your team or family and friends, and work out if you can adapt some of those great concepts to your own business. If they delighted and surprised you, chances are they will have the same effect on your own customers. Grab hold of the great, but be sure to avoid the tactics that put a frown on your face.

SOUNDS EASY! SO HOW DO I GET STARTED?

Your Observational Marketing kit should include:

- 1 notebook
- 1 camera / video recorder
- 1 pencil (a pen will do, but have a back-up for when it runs out from scribbling down all your observations!)
- 1 set of eyes and ears
- 1 agenda for your monthly marketing meetings

TUNNEL VISION

One thing about being an Observational Marketeer is that you will never switch off, even when you are on holiday or stuck in traffic. Game-changing ideas can strike at any moment so be prepared to write them down and act on them!

We live in South Tyneside, on the North East coast of England. It was whilst sat in traffic to enter the newly built Tyne Tunnel 2 that I had this creative idea to bring revenue into local councils whilst giving small business a massive kick-start to their marketing.

The resulting blog, which gathered great support on Twitter and Facebook, went as follows:

"Is it just me sitting in my Observational Marketing World thinking that our Councils are missing a great marketing opportunity here??

Just recently the second Tyne Tunnel has opened whilst the original is being revamped.

Right now local government is feeling the pinch and small businesses are feeling an even greater pinch on their purse strings and yet there is a quite obvious marketing solution here".

OB MARKETING IDEA #1

Sell the naming rights to the two tunnels!!!!! Stadiums have done this with the Emirates, Ricoh and Coca Cola arenas so surely the Tyne Tunnels can adapt this approach?

I am confident there is a car insurer, car manufacturer or car breakdown service giant out there that would love the opportunity to promote to thousands of motorists who drive through the tunnels every second of every day???

Historically the only piece of marketing taking place around the tunnel are billboards and frankly it is the most unimaginative form of advertising going when you pull up to the toll booth!

OB MARKETING IDEA #2

With the money raised from selling the naming rights half could go into the council budgets but some could be reinvested to help local businesses, and here is how I would do it....

At the north entrance there would be a large scale poster site that would promote the local area in a 'What's on' style of promotion for North and South Tyneside.

At the south entrance there would be another large poster site but this would be to promote local small businesses (BTW - this would be free due to the amount made on the naming rights).

A tunnel marketing lottery could take place to pick business names out of a hat and give them a free weeks advertising on this poster site!!! Oh and one last thing...... the design contract would be given to agencies north and south of the river Tyne.

Not all marketing ideas come to fruition; you can't win them all.
But never tire of observing the world around you and searching for creative new ways to market your own business.

COWS DON'T REVERSE

I often hear *"We have an all-singing and all-dancing website; we have some brilliant marketing materials; we have adverts that shine out from the rest, but business is slow!"* My response is this: unfortunately you can never rely on marketing activities alone; you have to continually look at new ways to attract new customers. Don't hide behind a marketing strategy. Physically get out there, be noticed, and attract business.

Think of it like this: you are a farmer in a field, sitting on a stool, holding onto your bucket, patiently waiting for the cow to reverse up to be milked. You're going to be waiting a very long time for that cow to reverse into anything even vaguely resembling a milking position. You need to pick up your bucket, pick up your stool, and walk to the cow yourself in order to milk it.

Look around. Is it a bit quiet? It's time to go and find some more cows. Take a walk into the next field to find some more. If your marketing strategies are working for you, and you're providing a great service to get the cows mooing, hopefully there'll be some new cows waiting in your original field when you come back to it, as the word has spread across the fields. (For the record, I'm not calling your customers cows, and I've never seen a cow reverse.)

Before I started my own marketing business and later became a speaker, I was the marketing manager at a large motor retailer. During my time there I made it my number one priority to take the vehicles out to the customers in their own environments. I placed 4x4's at agricultural country shows, put small cars into supermarket foyers, and sports cars at sporting venues. The take up of test drives, brochure requests, and overall sales was phenomenal, and this success came because I didn't rely on the website and adverts; I took the brand directly to the customers.

Whatever your business and wherever you're based, it can take a long time before word of mouth really begins to spread. Getting out there and physically getting yourself and your brand known at networking events, shows, awards and meetings is a fantastic way to market your business. Remember: you are your best marketing asset!

IT'S A BIG ISSUE BEING TOM CRUISE!

Whilst speaking at a series of seminars in the East Midlands I visited Nottingham city centre. The mission: to see Brian Clough's statue! As a Sunderland fan, I had heard about the statue and was determined to see it and take a photograph. Having received friendly service and directions from a member of staff in Waterstone's, I headed towards the Town Hall.

On my way there, I passed a guy selling the Big Issue. Now, the usual Big Issue sales pitch goes along the lines of *"Big Issue! Big Issue, please!"*. Not this time. *"Hey, there's Tom Cruise!"* the guy shouted. I looked around; there's only me. I laughed out loud and said

"Nice one, but I don't think so. Apart from weight, height and looks, we are very similar, but not today, thanks". I continued my statue hunt with a smile on my face, and was still smiling as I took a picture of one of the country's greatest ever football managers.

On the way back to the car I made a detour and walked back up to the seller and bought a copy of the Big Issue, saying *"that's for the comment"*.

The moral of this story? Dare to be different; stand out, and make sure you're remembered. It might just get you the sale!

CHASE THE ACE

Ah, the humble business card! A brilliant yet so often overlooked piece of marketing. The business card is one of the very first pieces of marketing material that your customers will receive from you, so it needs to create the right image, be of the right quality, and be memorable. A lot to ask from a tiny piece of cardboard? Read on!

Whether your cards are in the hands of someone at a networking event or lying around on your client's desk, they need to shine out as proof that your business is offering the highest quality, and truly stands out from all the rest. So what makes a great business card, and how can you improve yours? The design, information, shape, and material are four of the most important points to consider.

THE DESIGN:
should be professional and clear, reflecting the quality of your business.

THE INFORMATION:
should highlight the key benefits of working with you, without overloading the card with text.

THE SHAPE:
is something you can really have fun with. Why not go for a die cut? This option is slightly more expensive, but will certainly get you noticed.

For my consultancy business, Mercury Marketing, I have a die cut around the Mercury wing and clients will always say *"Oh this is different"*, which is exactly the reaction I am looking for. Or how about a folded card? The extra space can be used for a mini brochure, price list, rewards card, calendar… My own folding card features some top tips and marketing ideas, and a tear-off card for referrals.

THE MATERIAL:

Just because it's called a card, does not mean it has to be made of card! What about using wood, metal, or cloth? If the material is relevant to your business then your card can be a great promotional ambassador. One of my clients has a pyrography business so we make his card out of wood with his contact details burnt into the material. Another example is a client who makes the emergency exit signs for ships, so passengers can find the exits should the lights fail on board. His business card is made from the same material – it glows in the dark! Have you ever thought of an edible business card? Yes, I have one of those too. It's made out of white chocolate and causes quite a stir, especially when I eat it on stage!

"PUT THE POWER OF YOUR BRAND IN THEIR HAND"

For me, I found the greatest business card in the world in Stellenbosch near Cape Town. I met Johan (he calls himself The Vine Hugger) and sampled some of his exquisite bio-organic wines from his award winning vineyards. He told me that everything they do 'goes back into the soil'.

Whilst sampling his produce I picked up his business card. It felt rough and bumpy: Not what I'd expect from a business card. However, when I turned it over it became the best business card in the world. Johan has embedded seeds into his business cards and if you plant his card, it will grow! Fully reinforcing his 'everything he does goes back into the ground' marketing, as anyone who plants and grows their business card will forever be reminded of where it came from.

THE EYES SHUT TEST

When thinking about the strength of your business card, try the 'eyes shut test'. Close your eyes and feel the quality of two different business cards, then ask yourself, still with your eyes closed: Which is the superior company?
Who provides the superior service? Who can I trust the most?
The answers to these questions will reveal which material quality you should choose. Remember: you can feel the quality of a business through its business card.

DON'T JUMP! IT'S A SLIPPERY SLOPE

There's an old marketing proverb that says *'Fish where the fish are'*. A little obvious, yes, but it fits just perfectly for these next two Observations which are all about placing your message in the right place at the right time for your target market.

When the severe weather in the UK restricts many businesses from fully operating, do you see problems, or do you see opportunities?

What if you were a cycling shop, operating in some of the worst snow storms ever seen?

Business would cease, right? Well, not for this opportunity spotting entrepreneur…

In the village of Barwick in Elmet near York there is a large bank which, when covered with snow, is a magnet for children and families who want to sledge.

The fluorescent sign (opposite bottom) was attached to the gate, to the bank… this sign is from a local cycling shop that has seen the opportunity to sell and so are advertising sledges, but most importantly they are *'fishing where the fish are'*: most impressive!

Where would you expect to find a message for people to contact the Samaritans? Yes, you guessed it, they are placed along the Tyne Bridge in Newcastle.

Fine Fettle Cycle are now selling

Sledges....!!!

Sliding Pan Sledge £4.99
Toboggan Sledge £14.99
Winter Gloves from £9.99

WHEN AND WHERE CAN YOU PUT YOUR MESSAGE RIGHT IN FRONT OF YOUR CUSTOMERS?

DOES SIZE MATTER?

We put a man on the moon, cure many diseases, break records, and constantly try to push ourselves to new levels, yet 99% of businesses promote themselves in the same way, shape and style. Why do so many brochures and flyers look like takeaway menus? Is it because they are easy to post or to display? Is it because they are cheap to produce? No. Ultimately it's because we just never think of doing anything differently.

On a trip to Stirling Castle (which is well worth a visit, I might add!) I noticed a brochure stand in the café area. Yawn. If your brochure is the same size, shape and style as every other brochure in the stand, how will your business ever catch the eye of your potential customers?

Jump out of the 10cm x 21cm box and think a little differently for your next batch of leaflets.

DIFFERENT SHAPES SCREAM FOR ATTENTION

As with business cards, a creative die cut flyer can be a great way of communicating your message differently. Die cut flyers are not all that common so they really stand out as they come through the letterbox or when they're in a shop, hotel or tourist spot. With an eye-catching, stand-out flyer, you're sure to be picked up first.

"ARE YOU THE IRONING LADY FLYER MAN?"

It's fair to say that I have become renowned for one particular marketing flyer. Of all the stories I share as a marketing speaker, the one that audiences always remember was created for a start-up business, many years ago. It's a concept that I am extremely proud of, so here it is…

Many years ago a client from the North East asked me for help in creating a mailshot flyer that would really grab the attention of her target market. The resulting flyer was so different that the concept and story rapidly spread around the rest of the country.

The business was an ironing service, and an initial promotion using A5 flyers hadn't produced any results.

So I took a pink sheet of A4 paper, added a strap-line and a business card, then crumpled the whole lot into a ball. These pink crumpled up bits of paper were then posted through letter boxes. What do you do when faced with a scrunched up piece of paper? – You open it, of course! Once the balls were unravelled, potential customers saw the strap-line *"Don't let your clothes become as creased as this".*

The response was amazing – in a trial drop of just 100 flyers we gained 8 new customers – an 8% success rate for a mail shot is unheard of!

So what could you do to make sure your potential clients pick up and read your message?

MAKING AN EXHIBITION OF YOURSELF

Why is it that so many exhibition stands look as though they have been designed by the Child Catcher from Chitty Chitty Bang Bang? What do I mean? Sweets! Everywhere! Do they actually attract and keep people at your stand for any of the right reasons?

Alongside the sweets there are the beautiful pop up banners, the laptop or tablets showing the company's website, a fanned set of brochures, and then the pens, coasters, mouse mats, memory sticks, rulers, rubbers, pencils, t-shirts, mugs, tote bags...

Now I may sound cynical here, and deep down there's nothing really wrong with any of these ideas. But take a moment to look around. How many of the other exhibitors standing around you have the same collection of branded giveaways? How many people have come over to your stall, picked up a pen and a handful of sweets, then wandered away without taking even a moment to find out who you are and what you do?

REMEMBER: TO STAND OUT WE NEED TO BE DIFFERENT. THINK ENGAGEMENT, THINK EXCITEMENT, THEN THINK ENGAGEMENT AGAIN.

How about a Scalextric track on your table which would encourage people to race around the track with the fastest time winning a prize? Or a video game with the highest score winning your products or services? (If you can get a game that relates to your industry, even better!) How about creating a coconut shy next to your stand, or a hook-a-duck style competition? These ideas may sound a little far-fetched, but can you honestly tell me you wouldn't want to participate in these ideas if you were walking past them? Increase the length of time delegates are engaged with your stand, and you're dramatically increasing your chances of making a great impression and being remembered.

Of course, your aim is to qualify leads when delegates visit your stand; to build a relationship in those few minutes so you can

hopefully go on to meet again and do business in the future. You and your stand should be the one piece of marketing that people will remember from their day.

A great example of this stand-out performance comes from the fabulous business Barefoot No More. On top of, and surrounding their exhibition table are hundreds of shoes. Based in South Africa, Barefoot No More give a child a pair of shoes for every pair of their flip flops sold. For 3 days this stand was the busiest at the Coca Cola Dome in Johannesburg.

ALL GIVE AND NO TAKE

Since becoming a dad, I've observed some great marketing practices adopted by some of the country's leading baby brands, namely Pampers, Calpol, Early Learning Centre, and Mothercare. They are possibly the most helpful brands I have ever come across.

How did they make us, as parents, take note? Here's how:

PAMPERS - every month we receive useful email updates with hints and tips on child development.

CALPOL - the greatest piece of direct mail, ever! They use our forenames in the main body of their promotional letters, featuring great hints and tips.

EARLY LEARNING CENTRE - our daughter, Grace, would like to say thank you for her FREE Animal Music CD which arrived from ELC a week before her 2nd birthday!

MOTHERCARE - Simply the best customer service, all round! Helpful, cheery and knowledgeable at all times. Once, after I'd finished delivering a seminar, a former Mothercare employee came over to tell me she received *'Employee of the Month'* for taking a bowl of water out to the car park for a customer's dog while the customer's car was being fitted with a child seat. I rest my case.

Marketing is about giving as well as taking, and a special mention must go to our local hospital and the staff who work there. Whenever we donate toys and books to the children's ward, we always receive a hand-written thank you note or card.

One key thing about these companies is that they never tried to sell us anything. They didn't send vouchers or special offers; they simply shared their expertise with parents, offering advice, giving gifts, or saying thank you. Many businesses could learn from these marketing techniques – marketing isn't solely about promoting and making sales; you also need to look after your customers, old and new.

Dear Hayley

Make Grace's first birthday Speci

It's Grace's first birthday soon, which is a huge milestone for both of you. So we want to help you make a real splash. That's why we've enclosed a little treat for now, as well as lots of ideas for the big day.

The treat for your baby to enjoy right now is a special *Under The Sea* CD. Try listening to it with your little one on your lap, and help them to move and clap along with the music. It's a great way to start getting them excited about music and rhythm.

20% off Grace's present

If you like you can carry this watery theme right through to the birthday party. There are plenty of gift ideas attached, and you can have 20% off all our toys and games with the voucher below.

A few games to make Grace's party go swimmingly

Having a few sleepless nights?

Lack of sleep is a natural part of being a new mum or dad. As well as having a tiny mouth to feed at all hours, you've probably got a million and one things on your min is Grace feeding enough? Is her room the right temperature? Is Geoff ever going to have time to clean the bathroom?

One of the most common worries at this stage is about illness. As the centre of attention with family and friends, Grace is bound to pick up a few coughs and

Tips for Mum

AND THEN A CELEBRITY WALKS IN ...

Ask yourself this simple question: What would you do if you knew an A-List Celebrity was planning to visit your business tomorrow?

I first explored this idea during a keynote talk which I delivered in Cumbria. I asked the audience *'Do you treat every customer the same?'*, and one lady shouted out an emphatic 'Absolutely!'. I then asked her, 'What if that customer was an A-List Celebrity? What if Brad or George's agent called to let you know they'd be popping in, tomorrow?' She thought for a moment, then said she'd probably do a little more for them – polish the floors, get a hair-cut, make sure she was dressed to impress, get some fresh coffee...

I'm sure many of us think we are offering a consistently high level of customer service to every single one of our clients, but the fact remains that if a true *'A-Lister'* were to visit us tomorrow, we'd find ways to treat them just a little better than the rest.

WHAT WOULD HAPPEN IF YOU WERE TO TREAT EVERY CUSTOMER LIKE A CELEBRITY?

Think of the word of mouth publicity that could generate, and at surprisingly little cost! The celebrity service technique involves making some simple upgrades to the things you already do.

For example:

NORMAL VS CELEBRITY
Customer Service	Customer Service

NORMAL Customer Service	CELEBRITY Customer Service
Instant coffee	Fresh coffee
Plastic cups	Branded mugs/china cups
Business hours	Flexible times to suit them
Uniform	Your best suit & polished shoes
Proposal emailed within a week	Proposal hand-delivered

Now make your own list of how you look after your customers and see where you can upgrade the level of your service. You may be surprised how much you can do to delight your customers!

GOING BANANAS

How do you make your clients or customers feel special? How do you make them leave your premises feeling at least two inches taller? Well, one simple way is to give them a great compliment...

It was the last day of our holiday in New York; we had a few hours to kill until our flight, so we were sitting outside Grand Central Station wondering what to do with ourselves. The light bulb moment came, and seconds later we were inside Banana Republic, trying to rid ourselves of the remaining holiday dollars that were burning holes in our pockets.

Hayley turned left towards the ladieswear, and I turned right. I picked up various items of clothing and entered the changing room, trying on a white t-shirt and a sweater...

As I opened the door a member of staff was rushing through with a pile of clothes up to her eye balls. With her load of clothes, she hit the door, causing it to swing open with my hand still attached.

Three paces later the shop assistant stopped, turned around and pointed: *"that sweater looks fab on you!"*

Shocked, stunned, ego inflated, I left the changing rooms feeling 2 inches taller.

Now am I the only sucker for a compliment? I, of course, went on to buy the t-shirt, sweater, and the same sweater in a different colour (I do hope that shop assistant meant it!).

EQUATION:
Compliments = Feeling Great = Buying More!

So how can you make your clients feel great and leave them feeling two inches taller?

ICEBERG AHEAD

If you really want to stand out from the crowd, Ice Breakers are for you! An Ice Breaker is a wacky gimmick which is posted or delivered to your target audience, along with a card or covering letter with an ice-breaking message. Its main aim is to cause a stir, a surprise, or a smile, but most of all it's about getting your brand to register in the recipient's mind.

So what could you do? Here are some ideas that brought great success to the companies that used them:

USING YOUR LOAF

I created an ice breaker for P3 Coaching a Newcastle-based coaching company. We delivered small loaves of fresh bread, delicately wrapped in pink tissue paper, and placed inside white paper bags – the client's brand colours – to the offices of their target audience. The covering letter carried the strap-line *"The best thing since sliced…"*
The result = the seminar was fully booked.

GETTING YOUR FOOT IN THE DOOR

To promote a training company we placed a child's running shoe in a small shoe box and sent these boxes to targeted recipients with a marketing letter. The ice-breaking message: *"Have you been looking for the right trainer?"*
The result = appointments were made and contracts won.

PUCKER UP

To sell used cars, after the launch of the new 51 plate change in the UK I sent out a promotional mailer to a database of customers with a plastic piece of mistletoe, and the message *"Kiss goodbye to your car this Christmas"*.
The result = test drives were taken and sales soared.

I also received an Alfa Romeo comb in the post. Promoting the launch of their convertible Spider model. It simply said: *"You're gonna need one of these"*.

Of course I have my own ice-breaking tactics, too. When promoting my speaker business I send a pair of socks embroidered with my name and website. These are sent to prospective clients with a hand-written note and business card which reads on the reverse: *"Discover an inspirational marketing speaker to knock your socks off…"*

Once you've got your ice-breaking idea, send your material to your target audience, and be sure to follow up within a week. If you can start the phone call with *"Hello there, did you get your…?"* you've instantly warmed up what might otherwise be a cold call – they're bound to remember you, and the ice has been well and truly broken, opening up the conversation to discuss how you can work together!

REMEMBER: THINK GIMMICK; THINK COST EFFECTIVE; TEST, MONITOR AND TWEAK IF NECESSARY. LET ME KNOW HOW YOU GET ON!

AND THE WINNER IS...

This technique ticks off some great marketing boxes, and is completely free! Entering yourself and your business for an award is a fantastic opportunity to really showcase your strengths and the true quality of your products or services.
Business awards are run by all sorts of organisations including business support agencies, local councils, banks, business networks and industry groups, locally, regionally and nationally.

You will need to take time to study the questions and entry criteria before completing your entry form, but just imagine if you were to be shortlisted or if you won! What could you gain? Well, let's start with the great **FREE** press coverage you can use to raise your profile. Then there's the logo or badge for the awards event which you can feature on your website, newsletter, emails and marketing materials. And of course, once you've won, there'll be

your shiny new trophy or plaque to put in pride of place in your reception area for all to see.

The awards nights themselves tend to be fantastic events and offer a great opportunity for networking with other successful businesses. How about booking a table at the event you've been shortlisted at and taking some of your valued clients along for the evening?

By far the most prestigious award I've received was when I was voted best speaker at the World Advertising Forum in Tehran, Iran. Not only had 2,000 people in the audience voted to give me this accolade, but the prize I received was a beautiful hand-made Persian rug. And it's not just about being crowned the winner; it's also about what you can do with it after the ceremony. As you can see, I've had numerous articles written about me and my Persian rugs, and of course it's on my email signature and business proposals. Leveraging your award win can be a priceless way of promoting you and your business.

Remember, whether you win or not, there's always a positive story to be gleaned from participation in an awards event - be sure to shout about it in the press and in all your marketing efforts!

OMG - How about taking the promotion of your awards even further... If you ever walk along Ocean Road in South Shields you will come across a host of fish and chip restaurants, pizzerias and curry houses, but if you were an award winner how could you bring a sense of extra credibility and added competitive edge.

Colmans Fish & Chip Restaurant have had a brown sign added to the end of the street so every tourist can see that they are the ones with the better fish & chips!!!

GLOBAL PRIZE FOR RAMM IN IRAN

A South Tyneside marketing speaker and entrepreneur has won a prestigious accolade in Iran following a tour of the country.

Boldon based Geoff Ramm, made the 6,000 mile round trip to Persia and was voted 'Best Speaker' at the country's First World Advertisement Forum in the Iranian capital of Tehran.

Geoff took to the stage alongside various other illustrious speakers from across the globe and wooed 1800 businesses in just two days with his keynote talk which was translated from English into Farsi.

Geoff said: "This was my first international speaking engagement.

Entrepreneur voted 'best speaker' in Iran

EPINAY MUST STAY

I am often asked *"What has been your greatest marketing achievement?"* and over the years I have had a few answers to this question as I have achieved and succeeded in new things. However, the story I'm about to tell you will probably never be beaten.

For several years now I have had the pleasure of working with Epinay Business & Enterprise School, helping them to market and promote their enterprise modules, namely their jewellery, organic garden and café. From designing creative menus and brochures to writing PR campaigns, the aim has always been to help raise the profile and awareness of the school.

One day, whilst sat in the Head Teacher's office the Head Mrs. Harrison passed me a letter from the local council. The letter was informing the school that it was under severe threat of closure, and that they would be relocated to a brand new, purpose-built school. Sounds great, eh? Not quite... unfortunately, the new school would not be able to accommodate all of the children, so some would have to go into mainstream education. You see, what I didn't mention is that Epinay Business & Enterprise School is a school for pupils with moderate learning difficulties and associated challenging behaviour.

Our usual marketing and promotional strategy meeting took a dramatic twist that afternoon as we turned our attentions to coming up with ideas to save the school. *"Epinay Must Stay"* was born.

Now back in the olden days if you wanted to save something you would pull together a petition, and rally around the local area gathering signatures to deliver to the council. What we came up with instead was a world first.

We created a 3 minute viral petition video with the children and uploaded it to YouTube. We then promoted the campaign on Twitter, Facebook and LinkedIn. After a short wait while the video hits climbed through social media channels, we released the story to the traditional media. Within minutes we had BBC, ITV, BBC Radio Newcastle, the Evening Chronicle and the South Shields Gazette featuring us on the airwaves, on screen, and in print.

The teachers, parents and pupils fought hard to save the school with meeting after meeting, and document after document, until, months later, I received the call from the school telling me the school had been saved. The marketing campaign played a big part in making this happen and it proves that when creativity meets opportunity great marketing happens!

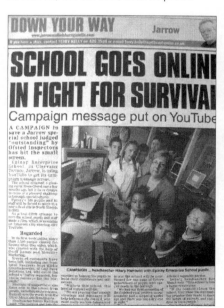

DRINK & DRIVE

If you are considering a new brand identity, new marketing materials, or a new website, here's a great technique for creating some really innovative ideas.

I often see businesses who spy on their competitors' websites and brochures for inspiration for their own marketing, looking to *'pinch'* the best bits from each one, then blend them together to create their own *'unique'* brand identity. Such regurgitation of what the competition has done is hardly the leap that's going to make you stand out from the crowd, though.

Now I would never advocate drinking and driving, but when it comes to creating marketing materials or an edgy new website, *'Drinking & Driving'* is an easy and creative technique to adopt. First, describe your business in just three words – fresh, funky, stylish; innovative, creative, cool; sexy, sleek, inspiring; traditional, precise, exclusive, etc.

Now take your chosen words and ask yourself:

If I were an alcoholic drink, which brand would I be?

If my business were a car, which brand would I be?

Think of the drink and car which most align with your brand's three descriptors.

Here's the easy part: visit the websites of those two brands and see how they do it. If you can, get hold of their brochures and other marketing materials. From this simple research you'll be able to adapt and tweak some of their ideas for your own business, creating materials that stay true to your brand but are completely different to the competition.

In case you're wondering, I am Honda and Carlsberg. Both are traditional and reliable, but very different and wacky in their approach to promotion and marketing.

TURNING NEGATIVES INTO POSITIVES

Why do so many businesses litter their space with negative posters and signage? What atmosphere does this create for customers? What sentiment does it inspire towards our service and brand? Wouldn't it be great to replace every negative with a positive?

At the Harrogate Christmas Arts and Crafts Fair there were many micro businesses promoting and selling their products to eager Christmas shoppers. Most tables were adorned with small paper and card signs saying *'Do Not Touch'*. Not so in the case of one stall selling beautiful, hand-carved wooden toys. The paper signs invited visitors at the stall to pick up and touch the toys, feeling the quality of the products in front of them!

Some other negative signs that we all see far too often include:

'We accept no responsibility for the safety of your vehicle or its contents' – thank you, that's very reassuring.

Probably the best (worst?) example I've seen of negative signage was spotted in a hotel in Sorrento, Italy. Crammed on to one noticeboard was a whole cloud of negativity: *'No Diving' (twice!), 'No lifeguard on duty', 'Night swimming is prohibited', 'No food around poolside', 'Pets not accepted'.* Hardly creating a positive feeling around the hotel!

Now take a look at how necessary messages can be delivered in a positive tone. Impressions retail store in the North East of England highlight on their changing room signs that they have both male and female changing rooms; that customers can take in unlimited numbers of garments, and that staff are on hand for assistance.

The lesson to learn?
Whether you're using negative wording in your signage, website content, marketing, or anywhere else, take the time to review how you're delivering your message and turn those negative words into positive ones so they inspire a smile, not a frown.

THINK LIKE A GLADIATOR

When General Maximus Decimus Meridius entered the Colosseum for the first time, he and the other gladiators stood in awe. Before the gates opened and the chariots charged into the arena for the first battle, Maximus turned to the other gladiators and said *"We've got a better chance of survival if we work together"*. We all know what happened next: gladiators from left and right gathered together in the centre of the arena and formed an impenetrable armadillo-style wall of armour.

Some gladiators chose to fight alone and were the first to be picked off by the chariots, while the group working together fought back and ultimately won.

FUSION MARKETING

Every day I see small businesses spending time, money and effort on promoting themselves and trying to take on the big guys. Much like the go-it-alone gladiators, they tend to be the first to get picked off. However, sometimes we see these small companies coming together - sharing their efforts, ideas, and investments, in order to take on the champions. This, ladies and gentlemen, is Fusion Marketing.

Fusion Marketing happens when like-minded businesses, with the same target audience, collaborate, promote and market together, sharing the costs of advertising, flyer production, and exhibition spend. By sharing these expenses they can cut what they're spending, or spend the same amount and multiply their exposure, targeting wider areas and massively increasing their potential customer database.

For examples of Fusion Marketing take a look at the flyers that come through your door in the next few weeks. Those A5 sheets of paper with a landscape gardener on one side, and the local garden centre on the other; the hairdresser and the beautician; the plumber and the joiner; the babysitter and the dog-walker. Now look at the flyers that are only printed on one side – who could those businesses partner up with to increase their exposure and cut their marketing costs?

I've seen some great examples of Fusion Marketing in recent years.

Squigglers – the children's fun painting club – got together with other local businesses including a soft play area, a swimming group, and a children's shoe shop. Together they created the Rainbow Reward Card so that every one of their customers could take advantage of a 10% discount at any of the businesses involved. The collective also targeted parents in the area, sharing the marketing costs to attract new business.

Then there was Anthony Holden from AH Holdens in Barrow in Furness who got together with like-minded home improvement businesses including builders, electricians and plumbers. They designed and distributed thousands of brochures to target home owners with details and offers of all their businesses – all for a fraction of the cost of being a lone gladiator.

Such collaborations are rare, but can be hugely successful, so think: who could I fuse with? And be sure to remember to fuse with people and businesses you can trust, as this will have a direct impact on your brand too!

A QUESTION OF BALANCE

Do you gather feedback from your customers and clients?
If you don't, you need to!

Collecting and acting on feedback is the only way you can really improve your service, delivery, staff training, and promotional strategies, and it's so easy to collect! It takes just moments to send out an email or post a survey after a customer has purchased from you, or to give them a call.

Remember when using questionnaires to keep them balanced. So many surveys sway the responder to give a positive grading, which is great for the ego, but doesn't always give an entirely accurate reflection. Make sure you balance each potential positive response with an equally negative one - if anything you're doing is terrible instead of great, you need to know about it!

Imagine if each of your customers were to give you one idea of how you could improve what you do. What value could that add to your business? Feedback is also a great opportunity for you to find out where your customers heard about you. This means you can assess your marketing strategies, make adjustments, and thank anyone who has referred you to others.

Remember, without feedback, you are always going to be guessing what your customer really thinks; unless you can actually read minds, it's always easier to just ask!

6. Overall

Taking everything into account:

	Excellent	Good	Fair	Poor
A Flights	☐	☐	☐	☐
B Holiday weather	☐	☐	☐	☐
C Resort	☐	☐	☐	☐
D Accommodation	☐	☐	☐	☐
E Representatives	☐	☐	☐	☐
F Holiday overall	☐	☐	☐	☐

Please tick one:	Excellent	Good	Average	Poor
Quality of food				
Quality of drink				
Speed of service				
Staff friendliness				
Menu selection				
Cleanliness of table				
Atmosphere/Comfort				
Value for money				
Presentation of food				

	Very good	Good	Fair	Poor
Sandwich quality				
Coffee quality				
Soup quality				
Quality of service				
Friendliness				
Cleanliness				

WARNING: The above questions are great for the ego!

I CAN'T GET NO SATISFACTION

**Have you got, or would you like to have, satisfied customers?
No? Good! If you answered *'Yes'*, I have some homework for you.**

Before you go home tonight, pop into your local supermarket and pick up some fresh ingredients for dinner, and a nice bottle of wine. Once home, cook your loved one a fantastic meal and chill or breathe the bottle of wine. Light some candles, put some romantic music on and enjoy the meal (you should definitely be in the homework mood by now!). Following the meal and wine, make love to your partner. Then ask them *'how was it for you?'* If they turned to you and said *'That was satisfactory'*, I imagine you'd be pretty disappointed!

You see, *'satisfied'* really just means average. It was okay; maybe a 5 or 6 out of 10. Do we really want to deliver such a mediocre service? From now on, remove the word *'satisfactory'* from your vocabulary and strive for something altogether more powerful and positive - leave your customers delighted, and amazed. Be fantastic!

COMMON COURTESY

Read any number of marketing books from the past 20 years, and the majority will tell you time and again to make courtesy calls to your customers. So why is it that I have received a grand total of 2 courtesy calls in the last 8 years?
It's a great tip which is massively overlooked these days. If no one else is doing it, what a great opportunity to stand out from the crowd and leave your customers delighted!

AN EGG A DAY HELPS YOU WORK, REST AND...

A few years ago we visited the City of York on Easter Saturday to meet up with some friends. It was a scorcher of a day and ice creams were a-plenty. Instead of driving home that night we decided to book in at the York Pavilion Hotel.

At 5am the next morning our daughter Grace awoke, bright and early, and we all got changed ready for a morning stroll. As I opened the hotel bedroom door, there by my feet was a Mars Easter egg. Wow! I had completely forgotten it was Easter Sunday, and as I bent down to pick it up I glanced down the hallway and noticed an egg placed beside every door. At this point I did think to myself *'we are the only ones up and out of bed… and we have a 4x4 parked outside… maybe no-one would know if we just…'*

No, of course we didn't, but I did think this was a great customer service idea. So much so, I rang the hotel later that week to tell them how great it was and how it was such a thoughtful surprise.
I also asked their permission to talk about it to audiences, and to write about it too.

They were delighted to have received the call and the manageress said I was the only person to have ever thanked them.

There are two lessons to take from this story: firstly, surprise and delight your customers (remember, this only cost them £1 per customer), and secondly, when you are surprised and delighted, make sure you contact the company to congratulate them and to thank them! They will keep doing it and the customer service snowball will continue to roll.

GHOST BUSTER MARKETING

Would you love your customer to think of your brand first whenever they are looking to purchase your type of product or service? Ghostbuster Marketing is all about being on the tips of the tongues of your customers; the first name that springs to mind when they're searching for your type of business.

Write down two makes of trainers – the first two that come to mind. I will attempt to do two things:

1. Guess the two you've thought of, and

2. Guess the order in which you thought of them

Over 90% of my audiences shout out Nike first, followed by Adidas. Why? These two brands are by far the most prominent and highly visible in their marketplace, using point of sale, viral marketing, direct mail, and sponsorship, among other activities, to stay ahead of the pack.

You may well have thought of some other brands of trainer – Reebok, K-Swiss, Puma – but the vast majority of us jump straight to Nike and Adidas every time.

So why is it called Ghostbuster Marketing? If you were looking to buy a pair of trainers, *'Who ya gonna call?'* - it's going to be Nike or Adidas – the brand at the forefront of your mind; sitting on the tip of your tongue.

Now you don't need the budgets of Nike or Adidas to create some Ghostbuster Marketing for your own brand; you just need to find creative ways to be consistently visible in your marketplace. Instead of sponsoring the Olympics or a football stadium, you can sponsor local school teams or tournaments; rather than spending a fortune on a full page advert in the press, run a competition or offer free samples to readers; offer to give a free talk to an audience at an exhibition, rather than buying an exhibition stand and hiding in the crowd. All these options involve relatively little outlay, and are guaranteed to get you noticed and remembered.

There are tonnes of cost-effective marketing activities you can undertake to get your brand known and remembered for all the right reasons. The key is to keep your message and visibility consistent – as soon as you stop there's an opportunity for your competitors to grab your spot on the floor!

BUSY BEE MARKETING PLANS

Businesses are busy!
Busy marketing, busy selling, busy buying, busy hiring, busy thinking of new ideas, and busy fire-fighting on a daily basis. In fact, they're too busy to find the time to plan the coming year's marketing campaigns and activities!

I regularly visit businesses and see many gloriously colour-coordinated wall planners on the walls in offices. But guess what they're used for. Plans? Targets? Ideas? Campaigns? Marketing strategy meetings? NO! I see holidays!!! A beautiful chart full of the staff's summer breaks, long weekends away, and golf trips!

It's so important to take specified time out of your business to sit down and plan your week's, month's, and year's marketing activities in advance. With some forward planning you can ensure that you always hit the print, delivery and follow-up deadlines, maximising the results from your marketing efforts.

Each month make sure you have a marketing meeting, either with your colleagues or, if you're a one man band, invite your business advisor and bank manager along.
Ask and answer the following questions as part of the core agenda of your meeting:

- *What have we done this month to boost business?*
- *What has not worked as well as we'd hoped?*
- *What will we do differently next month to increase our chances of success?*
- *How can we improve our service delivery?*
- *How can we stand out from the crowd?*
- *What are our targets for the coming month?*
- *What are the timescales for our marketing activities?*
- *Who has responsibility for each activity?*
- *What are we investing?*

Plot each event and deadline onto your wall planner, for the whole office to see. Use different colours for different activities e.g. press releases, direct mail, events & networking. When you reach a target – perhaps leads gained, sales achieved, or press coverage – give a silver star for the day or activity. When you exceed your targets, celebrate with gold. As time passes you'll be able to tell in an instant which strategies have worked and which haven't so you can make adjustments for the next year's plan.

So here's your shopping list for a simple, effective, visual plan that will keep you on track for the coming year:

A large wall planner
A pack of coloured pens
Some gold and silver stars

Remember: you plan your holidays, special events, and moving home. Make sure you plan your marketing with the same commitment!

This technique is a great motivational tool and can become incredibly addictive. Enjoy!

Christmas time is, of course, the time for giving, and it's a great opportunity to thank your customers and clients for their business during the year. What will you give during the festive season to make a lasting impression?

CHRISTMAS CARDS

For many years they were the most popular way to wish people a Merry Christmas, but they've been increasingly replaced with emails and online cards, sent to everyone in your contact list. As postage costs have increased, the sharing of traditional Christmas cards has shown a massive decline. I don't know about you, but I keep any Christmas card I receive for the full month of December, whereas I open and delete e-cards within seconds.

So how can you maximise your marketing potential with a traditional card? First, ensure your brand is on the front of the card, not inside it. This means your image or logo will be displayed for a full month in the office, reception area, or on the fireplace of your chosen recipient. Secondly, make sure you have your cards handwritten and ready to post so they arrive within the first week of December. That's a full month of prime exposure in the workplace of the recipient for the cost of a card and postage stamp – brilliant!

CHRISTMAS PRESENTS

You may have extra special customers and associates who you'd like to splash out on. A thoughtful gift is a great way to say thank you, and will ensure you are remembered. A bottle of wine or spirits, diaries and calendars are all fair ideas for gifts, but here are a few slightly more imaginative ideas:

Potted Plant
With a gift tag reading *'Wishing you growth for the coming year'.*

Lottery Ticket inside a card
With the message *'Thanks a million for your business this year'.*

Giant Cookie
'Wishing you sweet success for next year'.

Books
Business books you've read and enjoyed make a great gift for clients.

CHRISTMAS CLEANING

Another great job to do during December is your Christmas Cleanse. I don't mean the Christmas clean of the house or the office, ready for you to bring in a dirty tree, or the full body detox in preparation for all that food and drink you've got planned for the festive season. What I mean is the annual cleanse of your marketing database – you do have a database, don't you? Contact all of your customers and clients to wish them a Merry Christmas, thank them for their business during the year, and to ask them if their contact phone number, email and postal address details are still valid. This simple technique in December will ensure next year's marketing campaigns are green for go!

SEXY TEXT

Are you turning your customers on? Do they stop to read every piece of literature you release about your business, your products and your services, whether by flyer, email or on your website? If not, it's time to sex up your text!

Like it or loathe it, we all get turned on by sexy marketing text. Would you rather paint your living room 'brown' or the sexy alternative *'Latte Mist'*? How often do you order a white coffee over a Grande Cappuccino? By sexing up the names and titles of our products and services we intrigue the customer, and encourage them to keep reading (and get a little bit excited about it, too).

One of the best examples of sexy marketing text I've ever seen was in a famous department store in Newcastle upon Tyne when my wife and I were looking to buy a pram. We asked a member of staff to direct us to where the prams were and her response was sexy! She looked and smiled as she pointed towards the correct department: *"Yes, certainly. The travel systems are in the far corner"*.

And it didn't stop there! When we reached the 'travel system' department we found the pram we wanted with a sign on the handle which read "Free Climate Pack when you buy this travel system – worth £85" WOW! At this point I was beyond excited. Reading the words 'Climate Pack' I had visions of not only having the perfect travel system, but being one of the first dads to walk in the park with a Daddy Cool air-conditioned travel system – brilliant!

Unfortunately, the Climate Pack was not the air-conditioning kit I had imagined. The Climate Pack is sexy text for... wait for it... the umbrella for when it's sunny, and the plastic cover for when it rains!

Two more examples of brilliant sexy text came from Hyundai at the Coca Cola Dome (below) in Johannesburg.

And then there's the amazing Beefcakes Burger Restaurant in Cape Town, a gay burger restaurant. Their brilliant menu has fun with great titles and names for their products. From the *'Bugger The Burger'* section you could choose to order a *'Brokeback Special'*, or if you're not a fan of burgers, how about an *'All Gay Breakfast'*?

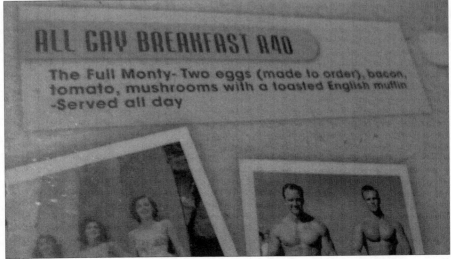

WHAT ARE YOU FAMOUS FOR?

These days, everybody wants to be famous, but as a business what are you actually famous for?
Being famous for something gets you noticed and talked about positively, and can be great publicity and word of mouth selling for you and your brand.

If you're ever in Newcastle upon Tyne, take a stroll along the wonderful Quayside and pay a visit to the geletaria, Risi's Ices. Inside you'll find amazing homemade Italian ice cream, pastas and paninis, but they are famous for something else; something no one else in the city has.

When I first met owner Mark Risi he showed me an old photograph that took my breath away. The black and white image featured the Risi ice cream van outside the current premises, with many cloth-capped customers staring into the camera. Amazingly, behind the ice cream van the Tyne Bridge had yet to be built! Risi are famous for their rich history, and no other business, including the large chains, can claim to rival such a heritage.

When we started working together we developed a brand image which mixed the current contemporary style with the rich heritage of the Risi brand. We used old family photographs to create themed artwork which now adorns the walls, giving customers the opportunity to read about and explore the history of the company. Customers are not only buying an ice cream or cappuccino; they're buying into a piece of 110 year old Italian and North East history.

If your business doesn't yet have a long history, start creating your own, right here, right now. If you want fame – and by *'fame'* I mean to be recognised and talked about for doing the everyday differently – the world is your oyster. So what could you become famous for?

Risi's celebrates its 110th anniversary

RISI'S ICE CREAM FACTORY

The Risi family have been serving up the cream of ice cream since 1898. Chris Robinson gets a taste of their history.

nebusiness

NEWS | DIGITAL | NOSTALGIA | STOCKS AND SHARES | FARMING

SPONSOR ME PLEASE

With such a plethora of marketing and advertising channels, how do brands target their markets? One creative way to put your name and products under the noses of potential clients is with sponsorship.

For example, how could a brand that targets families grab their attention for a full day? The answer lies within amusement parks which have become one of my favourite observation venues over the past few years, and they are becoming increasingly popular as marketing spaces.

Grace is now my co-pilot for the rides, and we have been on some great attractions both at home and abroad, but just take a look at how brands have exploded into the theme park arena. The legendary log flume at Alton Towers, Staffordshire has been replaced by the Imperial Leather bath tubs and ducks; the driving school is sponsored by Peugeot (they also have the family estate car parked at the entrance).

Sponsoring the next big attraction may well cost the earth, but there are numerous opportunities for you to get your brand out there.

Could you sponsor a table or award at a business awards dinner and invite your clients along?

Or what about sponsoring a local sport team or league and maximising the publicity opportunities associated with doing so?

Sponsorship isn't just for the big brands; find out where the opportunities are in your area, and find creative ways to get your brand known!

ONE NIGHT STANDS

Having met thousands of businesses across many sectors, it amazes me how few of them have a database of their customers' basic details: name, number, and email address. Businesses spend so much money, time, and effort attracting customers, then spend next to nothing on keeping in touch, and trying to attract those customers back in. Come on!!! This is basic marketing, but it's the basics that are so often overlooked.

I was once sat with a company owner who needed more business. I found out that they had served over 2,000 customers in the past year, but had never once contacted those customers with updates, offers or newsletters – nothing! I turned to them and said *'you are treating them like a one night stand'.* Doing all you can to attract them, you make the connection, do the business, and then you don't keep in touch… ouch!

Can you remember your last first date? You go out and have a great evening with a meal, drinks or the cinema. At the end of the night you say goodbye, hoping to see that person again, but you haven't got their number, email address, facebook… nothing.

The opportunity has been lost to continue the relationship, and many businesses treat customers like this. This has to stop.

Collect the data and keep in touch or you can forget about that second date.

Another question I am often asked is *'how many times should I keep in touch?'* Back in the days when I was marketing for Honda I was told it is best to keep in touch every quarter, but for me, the answer is simple… If you have something to say, say it; otherwise, keep quiet. There is no secret formula to suggest what your customers want to hear, and how often they want to hear it.

One of the greatest examples of keeping in touch I have observed is Sara Davies and her globally acclaimed Crafters Companion business. Whether they are at a trade show, appearing on TV, or gathering your details from the website from your purchase, they regularly send hints, tips, advice, offers and updates which their customers love – sometimes twice a week! This might sound like a lot, but because the content is of value to the receiver, her customers are more than happy to receive such regular communications.

Whether you decide to send out weekly, monthly or quarterly information, offers or advice, ensure it is of value to your customer, and be sure to ask for feedback on what they do and don't want to hear about.

SHAKING UP THE MARKET

You're launching the North East's first milkshake shop, and you want to excite children, students, and families into your new premises, create a stir, and get your brand out there.

How would you do it?

Shakeaholic, run by entrepreneur Ian Philpot, used social media to attract a younger audience to their new business. As the shop was being built and furbished, they handed out free samples, wrapped a car, ran news releases, handed out die cut flyers... But what really stood out was Maggie the Milkshake.

Standing at over 6 feet tall, Maggie captured the hearts of shoppers wherever she roamed.

This fantastic use of street theatre was seen around the Newcastle and Gateshead areas as Maggie the Milkshake successfully attracted hordes of customers to Shakeaholic's new premises.

FIGURE IT OUT

One of the most common problems businesses come to me with is: *"We struggle to put into words exactly what makes us different"*. Many businesses are constantly striving to describe their products or services in great new ways, but ultimately end up sounding just like the competition. We all know the buzzwords:

Unique
Forward thinking
Bespoke
Highest quality

...blah blah blah blah blah blah. These may sound great, but I look on them as 'waffle words', where sentences and then paragraphs are filled with nothing but waffle!

So when words fail you, how can you differentiate yourself from the competition? Easy: use numbers!

Here are 4 great ideas where you can use numbers to propel your point of difference into the customer's mind:

THE 1ST IS DESIRABLE DATES.

Have you got a date or a time which stands out from the rest? The best I have found so far is Kia with their 7 year warranty. While the majority of car manufacturers choose the bog standard 3 year deal, Kia came along and doubled it, then added an extra year for good measure, inspiring a serious sense of confidence in their brand.

THE 2ND IS IRRESISTIBLE OFFERS.

Think about the brilliant *"2 Dine for £10"* Marks and Spencer campaign. With just 2 words and 2 numbers they've successfully highlighted their special offer in a way that's easily recalled.

3RD IS
RESEARCH FINDINGS

This is a big favourite of mine. Every business, no matter how big or small, is currently sitting on a mine of great research findings. Just dig out the questionnaires and comment cards completed by customers *(you do do this, don't you??)* Costa Coffee, as the photograph shows, highlights research, but the best by far is 8 out of 10 cats prefer... Whiskas.

4TH IS
WACKY NUMBERS

It's great if you can make some stand-out statistical comparisons. Many years ago I helped to market a Slimming World franchise and we added up all of the pounds lost by the members. We found that the combined weight lost equalled that of a double decker bus!

A STRAW POLL

The art of outdoor creativity is being somewhat lost among the endless waves of digital and online messages, but this is still a sure fire way to attract attention. Every so often Mainsgill Farm Shop and Tea Room decorate their fields to grab drivers' attention as they travel along the A66.

I drove past this stunning piece of Outdoor Marketing during the general election in 2010. The farm had constructed four giant hay-men - depicting the three main political parties, and themselves.

Just a few weeks later, having seen the country create its first coalition government, they tweaked the hay-men in the field.

OMG!
THIS IS BRILLIANT!
THIS IS MARKETING!
THIS IS MAINSGILL!

USP x3

I own many marketing books – some great, some left unfinished. If there's one thing that has always astounded me in these marketing guides, it's description of the USP aka *'Unique Selling Point'* or *'Unique Selling Proposition'*, as they say across the pond. These books ask you *"What's your USP?"*, "Name your USP", suggesting you should have just one. This may have been relevant 20 years ago but right now I can buy online, offline and any line in-between. The choice of where and when, nowadays, is vast, so why should I choose to spend my money with you and your business?

My top tip is to ignore the one USP demand. Instead, write down three compelling Unique Selling Points that you have and your competitors don't. I call this the *right hook, left jab* and the *whack on the head* for the knock out. Based on the idea that your customer has three quotes or proposals in front of them, give them three great reasons to choose you.

Using my own USP x3 enabled me to work with NatWest in Cumbria. I was asked by the Business Manager: *"So what makes you the best marketing speaker then?"*. It was said in a friendly tone but I had to answer this question right if I wanted to get the job. First, the right hook: *"Every idea I'll be sharing with the audience tonight is under £1"*. The left jab: *"Each business will be able to use these ideas by tomorrow morning"*. The knock-out blow to the head: *"I use a 6ft skeleton called AIDA to relate your human body to your marketing activities"*. BANG! KABLAM! K.O!! The look on the Business Manager's face was priceless, and she said she would have to come and see me speak now, which she did.

Two weeks later I was booked to speak at an event for the NatWest Cumbria tourism clients on Lake Windermere. The 3 USPs secured this booking for me. The power of communicating in threes is sure to give you the edge over your competition!

GRIME TO GET CREATIVE

I have known about this technique for some time but had never seen it with my own eyes until recently. First, let me state clearly: it is illegal to graffiti. I repeat: it is illegal to graffiti. However, (and do check with your lawyers first) it is legal to clean up walls, fences and pavements!

On the way back to my car one day, I walked over this image of the Alfa Romeo Mito. Take a closer look and you will see that they have used a die cut template and cleaned over the top of the pavement to leave this image of the car.

Having spoken to Alfa Romeo they told me they had cleaned 1,500 pavements across the UK and created a great buzz surrounding their new stylish model via Twitter.

What could you do? Arrows to your café? Messages from a car park to your business to entice customers to follow to your premises? Do check first, but this is a great case of when creativity meets opportunity.

HAT TRICK HERO

I've had the pleasure of working with some great businesses in South Cumbria - Barrow and Furness, to be precise - on behalf of Furness Enterprise.

You may recall Anthony Holden of AH Holdens from Think Like A Gladiator earlier in the book. AH Holdens is an established window, door and conservatory business. Now, Anthony is a big Barrow football fan and whilst we were working together, Barrow were about to play in a Wembley Cup Final. How could he get his brand in the eye-line of thousands of supporters, and how could his brand be seen on ITV4 and in the regional press?

The idea was a simple one: we designed our own baseball caps, with Barrow FC on the front, and the AH Holdens logo on the back!

Barrow went on to win the final, and, as you can see in the photographs, AH Holdens were prominent at Wembley and will be forever kept as a souvenir!

So what big events are happening in your area? Where's the opportunity to display your business?

Following on in the same theme, this next idea was cheeky, but great nonetheless.

X MARKS THE OPPORTUNITY

Anyone remember Joe McElderry? You know, the X Factor winner? Like myself, Joe is from the good old town of South Shields.

During the X Factor final, the show came to the Temple Park Leisure Centre in the town to show live feeds of adoring and excited fans, including the Mayor!

Now this is a musical entertainment programme watched by tens of millions, and prime time advertising slots cost impressive amounts of money, so how could a radio station possibly get their brand seen by the millions watching, without paying for advertising or sponsorship?

Real Radio produced banners saying Go Joe, and gave them out to the audience.

The man who made these signs was Malcolm Lant from Signs Express, and he saw the opportunity to be creative once more when Little Mix and Amelia Lily were finalists. His brand was seen by over 18 million viewers!

IN A JAM

The Parc is a café situated in the picturesque coastal town of Cambrills in Spain. Whilst on holiday there we called in early one morning and ordered breakfast. We ordered omelettes, water, and Grace asked for a croissant with strawberry jam. We were the only ones there and the waiter seemed to be the only member of staff on at this time. 10 minutes later our omelettes and the croissant had arrived. We started to eat when Grace turned and said *"Daddy, where's my jam?"*; *"It will be coming soon, darling"*, I replied. 5 minutes later, no jam. 10 minutes later, still no sign, so I walked through into the café to find some.

To my surprise there was no-one there. The waiter had vanished. I called out: *"Hello? Hello?"* No response. I walked towards the kitchen; still nothing; empty! As I was about to walk back to our table, the kitchen door flew open and a large imposing person burst through in full black biker's leather, complete with blacked out helmet. He came towards me and I thought "&*$@ the place is being burgled". The guy lifted off his helmet - it was the waiter! He reached into his jacket and as he withdrew his hand he said, holding a jar up to me, *"Strawberry Jam"*.

It was a true *'Milk Tray'* moment; And All Because The Lady Loves......Strawberry Jam?!?!?

For me, this one instance completely rewrote the definition of customer service: *"Even if you don't have it, by hook or by crook, go out of your way and get it"*.

This guy was brilliant, and did we go back? Yes! Twice! And three times the following year!!

FREE & EASY

I am sure you'd agree that we could all do with some free and easy ideas to help get our product or service out there. Now to give away your products and services could be seen as detrimental in cheapening your brand, but there are some clever ways in which to spread your message.

Ted Baker clothing stores are the masters of service, with quirky marketing campaigns to boot. My first experience of this came at their store in Victoria Quarter, Leeds, back when I was at University. When I paid at the till they included a free condom with my receipt! Not sure what signals I was giving off with the shirt I had bought, but there you go!

I came across their quirky marketing techniques again some years later in London. As we walked into the store in Piccadilly Circus a member of staff at the front of the store asked us if we would like "Beer or Chocolate?" What?! So I took a beer (3 actually, as I was in there for an hour).

As customers walked in they were each offered a free Japanese beer called Kirin, or Ted Baker branded chocolate coins. This was a fantastic tactic for keeping customers in the shop for longer, and I'd be willing to bet money that Ted Baker didn't pay for the beer. In a great instance of Fusion Marketing, I would imagine that Kirin gave them the beer to give out as samples, fusing the beer brand's image with that of Ted Baker. It was a great sight to see people browsing the store with a beer hanging from their lips! Quite simply this is FREE & Easy to do, now who could you team up with?

On the same day in London copies of the book Witches and Wizards, by author James Patterson, were given away FREE to passers-by. Not only was it just before Christmas, so a great present for someone, but it was also at the time when this type of book was at its peak in popularity, so it was gratefully received by people walking past. Cleverly, the book also contained discount vouchers for other book titles in the James Peterson range, just in time for Christmas!

But what if your business is all online? Well we also subscribe to Lovefilm (when did we ever have time to drive to the video/DVD rental store??) who regularly send us vouchers for free months of movies – but these gifts are not for us – they're to give away to friends and family. This low cost tactic works by encouraging referrals, giving us a gift to give to someone else, at no cost to ourselves!

Freebies and sampling are as popular as ever now, but can you find ways to give it away without looking cheap or diminishing your brand?

SWEAT THE SMALL STUFF

I often read the phrase 'Don't sweat the small stuff, focus on the goal'. Well, when it comes to marketing and standing out from the crowd, I say 'You better sweat the small stuff, so much so that you will lose weight!'

Tintswalo are a stunning set of boutique hotels in South Africa, and are the most amazing hotels I've had the pleasure of staying

in – if it's good enough for Nelson Mandela, it's good enough for me! It's not just the rose petals in your room or the great personalised welcome at the airport that sets these hotels apart. It's their unique ability to listen to a miniscule piece of detail and then act upon it. While speaking for their management team I mentioned that I align my brand with Honda & Carlsberg. 8 hours later a knock on my bedroom door was followed by 2 members of staff quietly giggling to themselves, saying "We have drinks for you sir". I had not ordered room service so was puzzled. They walked in and left me an ice bucket …. (pictured below). But perhaps the most amazing thing for me was that they did not stock Carlsberg and had to go out and buy it!

I stayed in the Druids Glenn resort in Ireland and we've all seen the TV screen messages welcoming us to the hotel, but at this hotel they take the extra time and care to hand write the welcome on a note in your room. They also include a postcard (remember those?) so you can send a message about your stay to friends and family back home.

With a window seat secured for a 10.5 hour flight back to Heathrow I was looking forward to nodding off on the journey home. However, as I walked to my seat I noticed that I was in the middle of the plane. I asked the stewardess and she said there had been a mistake at check in and as the plane was full I could not move seats, but she did say she'd look after me. I was basically stuck. To the left of me was quite a large guy, and to the right of me an empty seat.

8 minutes before take-off (I was praying 'please close the flight now') another large guy with broad shoulders walked up the aisle; he was the only person left and was heading for the only spare seat on the plane, next to me. As I looked up I saw that it was non-other than ex England international footballer and legend of the game, John Barnes, who was going to be sitting next to me. After a few minutes of talking football – what else? – the stewardess hurriedly made her way towards me, leant over and said *"There's a window seat in 36a, it's yours if you want it, but you have to go now"*. What am I to do, sit beside the magician of the Maracana, or get some extra room and sleep? I said my goodbyes to John and headed to 36a. People say he was never comfortable on the right hand side but for the next 10.5 hours I think he was!

From today please take the time to sweat the small stuff; listen and act, get personal, and deliver on your promises. You never know, an Observational Marketeer may write about you one day!

UPSELLING ARNIE STYLE

This is one of my favourite stories and one of the greatest examples of up selling I have ever witnessed.

Up selling is all about adding extra value at the point of sale, whether it's done when taking an order, delivering the bill, or at the till. This is something we need to do to add greater value to each individual transaction, maximising our sales potential.

We landed at JFK and dropped our bags at the hotel before setting off for Times Square in the early evening, determined not to waste a minute of our holiday. We were feeling hungry, and as we're both big movie fans we decided to head for Planet Hollywood. We were welcomed by a friendly member of staff who walked us to our table. As she guided us through the restaurant she asked if we were visiting for business or pleasure.

My wife told her 'pleasure' and that it was her birthday. The waitress said "Congratulations and happy birthday!" – Nice touch!

We sat down opposite Arnold Schwarzenegger's jacket from The Terminator and ordered our starters, mains and then sweets – the staff sang Happy Birthday in between mains and desserts! Towards the end of the night we decided to delay requesting the bill and ordered one last drink each, including a cocktail for my wife. With a quarter of our drinks left the waitress came over and we asked for the bill. She said *"Sure"* and then, to my amazement, asked *"would you like to buy the glass as a souvenir of your time here at Planet Hollywood on your birthday?"* I was gob-smacked! I couldn't believe we were being up-sold! The waitress had cleverly used the information she had collected

about us at the beginning of the night to help her up sell at the point of purchase!

Of course, you can guess what happened next: *"oh yes!"*, and there we have it, we are now the proud owners of an $18 cocktail glass!

Ask yourself this simple question: do you know exactly why your customers have come to see you today?

Do you know who they are buying for, why, and what their specific requirements are? Only by asking the questions can you collect the information to help you up sell to your customers.

RAMM IN IRAN

My quote *'When creativity meets opportunity, great marketing happens'* could easily be dedicated to Iran and here are my 3 favourite observational stories from that wonderful country...

Myself and my speaking colleagues Sepehr Tarvardian, Kim Walker, Tony Anderson and Chris Arnold arrived in Mashhad from Tehran in the early hours of the morning. Bleary-eyed, we walked through the automatic doors to collect our luggage. As we walked through the doors we came across two ladies dressed in red suits, who were handing out fresh red roses. *'What on earth is this?'* I wondered. They were welcoming us to their city with the rose and attached to the rose was a flyer...

promoting their local restaurant. Brilliant! Can you imagine walking through arrivals at Manchester, Glasgow, Heathrow, or anywhere else for that matter, and a local business standing there at midnight with a gift to welcome you?

In the heart of Tehran, rush hour lasts for approximately 23 hours, so taking short cuts to the venues and hotels is a necessity. Imagine being parked up in traffic for up to an hour, slowly creeping forward, inch by inch.

This observation took place on the way back to our hotel. In the distance, a man with a hat walked up to each car, knocked on the window, opened a white box, closed it, and walked back to his shop front. This man had spotted the opportunity to promote his business to the frustrated drivers slowly passing by his premises. He was giving away a slice of pizza to every motorist during rush hour to promote his business.

After 2 weeks of touring 4 cities with 8 talks in 4 conferences, we all returned home quite literally exhausted. One week later a large parcel with Farsi text arrived at my home in the UK. Well wrapped, it took some time to open it. Inside was a personalised letter from one of the main sponsors and a good friend, Ali Jooya. It is customary to award the best speaker at the conferences with a hand-made Persian rug and I am proud to say I have four of these at home, but this rug was different. This rug was a children's rug, not for me, but for my daughter Grace! Thank you, Ali, you are a true gentleman.

NEW YORK
YORK
NEW YORK

Whilst visiting New York I visited a local café bar where I observed them selling fresh porridge with assorted toppings of fruits and syrups. Busy office workers coming into Manhattan would visit the breakfast counter and pick up some porridge to take away with them – a great and healthy option.

Fast forward to a great little café in South Shields – Coffea Caban. The owners wanted to open up earlier and bring in the breakfast trade. I told them about the take away porridge I had seen in New York, and we decided to launch 'Porridge to Go'.

We approached the local newspaper, offering every reader a FREE cup of healthy porridge. The editors loved the idea, and we gained three quarters of a page of free advertising! And all of this came from an observation on the other side of the world.

WHAT COULD YOU DO?

Offering your product or service to a radio station, newspaper or business journal can be a great way to get some free publicity and get people talking about you and your brand.

KNOW YOUR OATS!

Free porridge for every reader

COFFEE shop bosses are urging people to start the day the healthy way – with a nutritious breakfast.

Louise and Ewan Murray, owners of Coffea Caban in South Shields, have launched a new home-made Porridge-To-Go menu.

Their inspiration comes from across the Atlantic in New York, a city famous for its hearts on-the-go breakfasts.

Workers and tourists arriving in Manhattan via the ferry, tube and bus service start their day with a healthy, warming breakfast.

During the ice cold winter months, the Market Place coffee shop has teamed up with the Gazette to help you do the same.

Simply cut out the coupon and help yourself to a free portion of porridge, sure to warm the cockles of any commuter. There are three styles to choose from

By ANGELA TAGGART
Chief reporter

Classic Porridge, made with Scottish rolled oats, the fruity Ravishing Raspberry and Banana Bonanza, which is topped with freshly sliced banana.

Mrs Murray said: "We all know that breakfast is the most important meal of the day, but not everyone has the time to prepare or eat in the morning.

"Therefore, people arrive to work on an empty stomach and snack until lunchtime.

"Customers come in from the ferry and bus station and order a latte or cappuccino to walk to work with, but we wanted to offer everyone an extra healthy alternative that would warm you up on a morning.

"Home-made porridge is a great way to keep in shape after the Christmas holidays, and is a warming alternative to sandwiches and cereals."

The free porridge offer is available any Tuesday, Wednesday or Thursday during the winter months.

angela.taggart@northeast-press.co.uk

FACTfile: PORRIDGE

PORRIDGE is great at this time of year because it is high in Vitamin B6, which promotes the brain chemical serotonin.

High levels of serotonin are associated with feelings of well-being, while levels dip when sunlight is limited, which can lead to Seasonal Affective Disorder.

Porridge oats are high in complex carbohydrates and soluble fibre, which means they release energy slowly.

A bowl of porridge should provide all the energy you need until lunchtime.

HOT STUFF ... Louise and Ewan Murray, owners of the Coffea Caban, tuck into a bowl of porridge. (IRN 390452)

your free winter warmer

Coffea Caban

FREE fresh home-made Porridge-To-Go

Gazette

Market Place - South Shields

THE SHIELDS Gazette

Monday, February 19, 2007   www.southtynesidetoday.co.uk   38p

HOT STUFF
FREE COFFEA CABAN PORRIDGE – Page 15

ROEDER EYES DAVIES SWOOP
Back Page

SWEET SUCCESS

"Advertising does not work" and **"it's a waste of money"** are two of the most common comments I hear from businesses who have ventured down this promotional avenue.

Yet we've seen on-going advertising, from the early billboards in Pompeii to the banner adverts on web pages and social media, so surely some of these adverts must work, and increase the sales of the businesses who use them?

Here are a collection of hints, tips and ideas for you to consider before placing your next advert.

SWIM AGAINST THE TIDE

When everyone is going the same way, go against the flow – people may just spot you! I created this idea for Simply Chocolate, a chocolate and sweet shop, after they purchased a credit card sized advert slot in a local paper. To get the most from such a small space on a busy page, I knew we had to do something different; something unique. I came up with the idea of turning the text and offer upside down, knowing that every other business on the page would stick to the norm. The advert we created caused such a stir that it was picked up by a local radio station in the North East who spoke about it over the airwaves!

WHAT'S YOUR OFFER?

Why should YOU take action now? Without an offer, pretty much nothing happens.

ATTENTION GRABBERS

Capture people's attention in the offer with words like *'FREE'*, *'Exclusive'*, *'Last Chance'*, or *'Hurry'*.

LESS IS MORE

It's commonly believed that whatever size of advert we buy, we must fill every millimetre of it in order to get value for our money. If everyone else is adopting this tactic on a cluttered page, the one with the clear space around the text will stand out from the crowd. Remember: less is more!

WHAT'S YOUR CALL TO ACTION?

Tell people what they need to do next: call for a brochure…; download for free…; register today by…

ENCOURAGE A SPEEDY RESPONSE

Place a limited time offer on your advert: *'Offer ends 4pm Sunday'*; *'Only 150 remaining'*; *'When they're gone, they're gone!'*

NEGOTIATE

Most advertisers try to sell you rate card prices – always make sure you barter and reduce the cost of your advertising spend, either receiving a reduced price, or a larger advert for the same amount.

PROBLEM SOLVER

What problem do you solve with your product or service? Customers want an easier life, so make it easy for them to see why they should buy from you.

DOING IT FOR THE KIDS

As children, we love excitement and engagement. We love surprises and the unexpected. We love to be in on the secret. Quite simply, we love to be involved. So if your business is looking to attract parents and their children, these marketing ideas are especially for you.

Observed and enjoyed at the Crowne Plaza hotel in Marlow – a children's check-in desk! A brilliant idea to keep the kids entertained while the grown-ups queue and check-in following a long drive in the car.

I observed what I consider to be one of the best shop fronts in the world in Barcelona at the amazing Imaginarium children's shop. Take a close look at the picture opposite.

There is, of course, a door for adults, but there's also a small door just for children... now ask yourself: as a child wouldn't you just love to walk through your own little door?

Is Spain the home of the children's door? Inside the Woody Woodpecker themed room at Portaventura there's even a children's door leading to the bathroom.

RECORD BREAK

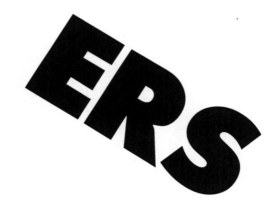ERS

We'd all love to create the most talked about event in town; the marketing story that captures the attention of local and national media; the idea that wins over the hearts and minds of your customers and attracts hordes of new ones. But how do we do it?

Now, I'd suggest you steer clear of the 100m sprint – that one's pretty competitive! But let's look at your products and services. Could you create or break a world record, based around what your business is already doing?

What if you were a baker? What's the largest scone in the world? Or the longest sandwich in the world?

A graphic designer? What's the record for memorising logos? How many logos could you create in one hour for new businesses?

Are you a personal trainer? What's the longest Zumba class? Could you hold the world's longest or largest training session?

All you need is an idea. Then plan the event; invite your customers, friends, family, the press, local businesses; promote it in the newspapers, on the radio and on television. Pretty soon your business could be listed in the Guinness Book of Records – just think what publicity and press coverage you could achieve with a record-breaking story!

MARKETING QUIZ:
SKY'S THE LIMIT

With so many methods available for communicating your business message on the move, how will you stand out and capture the eyes and ears of your customers?
Bus advertising? On the big screen at the cinema? On the metro? Bus stops? Taxis? On the side of bike wheels?

Q. Just along from the Parc café in Cambrills, Spain, your target market are soaking up the sun on the golden beaches. How do you attract these teenagers to your night club venue? Flyers, posters?

A. With your rivals competing at ground level, why not take your brand and message to the skies? As a child I used to crick my neck to observe these great pieces of marketing, but we rarely see them these days. Until Pacha nightclub decided to stand out from the crowd…

FROM ME TO YOU

One of the biggest traps businesses fall into is talking about themselves. The first page on every website is *'About Us'*; marketing letters and e-shots start with *'We'*, and brochures begin with *'Our Services'*.

Do you remember your last first date? Where you went? What you wore? Most importantly, can you remember the conversation? Imagine if your date had spent the entire evening talking about nothing but themselves – what they do, where they live, how many pets they have, what they had for breakfast that morning, where they went to school, what they did last week, every holiday they've ever been on... yawn, yawn... on and on... Would you go back for a second date?

If you're constantly telling your customers all about you, you're not offering them a chance to engage with you. When you talk about we, me, I, our, or us, you're not connecting with your audience; you're talking at them, not conversing with them.

SO HERE'S WHAT YOU DO:

Just like on a date, put your customer first. Instead of saying *'Our services include x, y, and z'*, remember the 'From Me to You' rule: *'You will receive x, y, and z from our services'*; *'You can benefit from x, y, and z'*; *'X, y, and z were designed for people just like you'*. Help your customers to feel connected to you and your brand.

M&S did this to great effect, changing their brand from M&S to Your M&S – brilliant!

WIN LOSE OR DRAW?

The month before Grace's 4th birthday I entered the toy mecca that is Hamleys Toy Shop, London. Now it's frequently said that retail is on its knees, but at Hamleys they do something different to everyone else: they demonstrate! Yes, that's right; they actually take the toys out of the box and show you exactly how great they are!

I arrived in the girls' toy department and proceeded to walk around. An easel, surrounded by children and their parents, stopped me in my tracks. Beside the easel was a member of staff demonstrating a new painting product on the easel. The audience were hooked and at the end when people had bought and left, the girl who had led the demonstration looked at me and asked a *'killer sales question'*: *"Would this be for anyone special?"* I said that it was for my daughter who loves to stick, glue, cut, paste and paint. She asked if I would like one but I said I'd have a walk around first and then come back.

So then the second killer question was delivered, *"What's your Daughter's name?"* I answered and then Julia, the demonstrating member of staff, proceeded to paint the name Grace on the paper and said *"If you don't come back and buy then please give this to Grace from me for her birthday!"*

For me this is all about personalising just about everything you do for your clients and

customers. One thing you can easily do is to personalise your future proposals.

I did this not long after meeting Julia and have seen a 20 per cent increase in sales. I am more than happy to share the before and after proposals with you, just drop me an email direct at geoff@geofframm.com

Oh, and just for the record, I bought the paints!

I have also promoted Julia and Hamleys ever since.

VIRUSES ARE GOOD

As social media websites have increasingly taken over our communications landscape, viral marketing, joke emails, funny videos, and online competitions have become powerful marketing tools for innovative businesses to promote their brands, products and services.

Free sites like YouTube, Facebook, Twitter, and Pinterest have created a new global arena for businesses to promote themselves, but how do you make yourself heard among the billions of posts made every day?

Viral marketing campaigns encourage the sharing of great videos, stories, and images between friends, family, colleagues, and followers, thus spreading your brand name and message.

I observed a viral marketeer, who said that for a viral to take hold it must stimulate our senses. The video, image or competition must make us laugh, cry, or shock us, forcing us to connect with the message and brand behind it. Would Britain's Got Talent star Susan Boyle have reached the same level of global fame without YouTube, Facebook, and Twitter? The coverage she got from 'shocking' our senses was incredible.

So what can you do as a business? Can you make a funny homemade video of your shop or staff? Could you create a great competition to share through your blog, Facebook, Twitter account, or YouTube?

Fellow speaker, Steve Spangler, is the architect behind one of the greatest pieces of viral marketing I've ever seen, that has taken the world by storm. I don't want to spoil it for you, but go and buy a packet of Mentos mints, and drop a couple of them into a two litre bottle of Diet Coke. Now stand back. This viral video has reached such levels that if you start typing 'Diet Coke' into Youtube, it will predict the word Mentos for the rest of your search. Great fun for kids' parties. Enjoy!

Who knows where your brand name could end up, but social networks are here to stay so you need to decide whether to jump on and enjoy the ride, or sit back and watch the competition romp away from you.

NAKED
AMBITION

There's no question about it: sex does sell - but it's nudity and flesh that really grab the headlines.

I have long admired the world famous Calendar Girls who saw the opportunity to do something creative in order to raise money for Leukaemia and Lymphoma Research. By stripping off in an 'Alternative Women's Institute Calendar' they raised millions for charity, and their story was later turned into a Hollywood blockbuster. Their efforts sparked a trend for nude calendars which have been adopted across many organisations, sectors, and industries looking to raise funds for their own charities.

Another of my favourite stories comes from Spanish clothing brand, Desigual. The first 100 customers through the store doors could walk away with a complete, FREE outfit, IF they showed up semi-nude. Cue hundreds of eager shoppers lining up outside stores in their underwear, and a massive amount of national and international coverage for the brand. Those that weren't among the first 100 in the queue were offered great discounts on their shopping for the day.

Now, I wasn't in the queue myself, nor did I walk past to see the story unfold, but I did hear about it on a national radio station some 300 miles away, and the promotion was such a success that Desigual have repeated the stunt in several other countries and stores!

Of course, nudity may not be right for you and your business, but rest assured, if you can bring this cheeky approach into your campaigns you're almost guaranteed an explosion of publicity!

WILLS AND KATE

The Royal Wedding in 2011 opened up a world of creative marketing opportunities for innovative businesses, both large and small. So just who were the marketing winners at the wedding of the 21st Century?

Supermarkets filled the aisles with Union flags and table cloths, party food and Pimms.

T-Mobile created a fantastic wedding spoof viral video which was viewed by hundreds of thousands of people.

Legoland Windsor created their very own Royal Wedding out of Lego, gaining great exposure in the process.

And what about Cumbrian graphic designer, Lydia Leith? Sick of hearing about the Royal Wedding, Lydia designed and produced *'Royal Sick Bags'*. Available in red or blue, with the title *'Throne Up'* across the top, these fun bags soon caught the attentions of the radio, television and press, and she sold thousands of her sick bags all over the world.

THRONE UP

ROYAL WEDDING

SICK BAG

KEEP THIS HANDY ON APRIL 29TH
2011

MARKETING QUIZ:
FREE WOOL

Is there such a thing as baad publicity? Well yes, of course there is, but this next observation is all about the power of your offers.

To attract customers to act on your advert you may well create a special offer: an introductory offer; one for the early birds; for a limited time only; BOGOF; 3 for 2... the list goes on. But my challenge to you, right here, right now, is.......

"Can you create an offer that is talked about in your area, or in your region, in your country or, wait for it... throughout the world?"

Q. A small retail outlet in Israel created just that by offering something that grabbed the attention of the world's media. This retail outlet was looking to drive up the sales of their televisions and white goods. In their position, what would you offer to get the punters in the door?

Perhaps an extended warranty, a discount off their next purchase, or a free DVD player? These are all great offers, but hardly likely to gain you coverage the world-over.

A. This outlet both wowed and shocked their customers and the world by offering a FREE SHEEP with every television or white good sold!

Aimed at Israel's minority Arab population, this promotion was run during the Muslim festival of Eid al Adha, drawing on the tradition for slaughtering a sheep during the festival.

To watch the video and see the amazing worldwide publicity buzz this offer created simply type *"Israel Free Sheep"* into your search engine.

By stepping out of the standard electrical marketing box, this small business gained worldwide coverage. Now I'm pretty sure you wouldn't get away with giving away a sheep with your products – animal protection services might have something to say about that! – but what could you offer to really make your business stand out?

WORLDWIDE DOMINO EFFECT

Fellow speaker and friend Kim Walker (an Australian) **hands me** (an Englishman) **a newspaper article** (in Iran) **about an** (American) **company who are celebrating 25 years in business** (in Japan).

The business was Dominos Pizza, who were celebrating 25 years in Japan.

To celebrate they did something incredibly different, offering the job of a lifetime: the lucky employee would get to work for just one hour in their company at a rate of $31,000 dollars per hour!

The news of this fantastic offer rapidly spread across the planet, creating a massive positive buzz around the Dominos brand.

In return for their offer of $31,000 and a few marketing costs, Dominos generated mass-hype around the brand and received priceless coverage in the media – a great return on their investment, achieved by thinking outside of the pizza box.

TAKE YOUR BAT & BALL HOME

Sun cream applied, listening to your Walkman (okay your iPod/MP3) **relaxing in the sun, and then, out of nowhere, a Rolex is thrust into your face, or a D&G belt, or a pair of Ray Ban sunglasses. If you've never been to Spain or Greece, this is the sales custom that awaits you - weary looking sales people, pounding the grains of sand all day to sell you what they think you want.**

Having already established the need to fish where the fish are, we should also take a look at the bait we are using. At the beach, we could agree that sunglasses are good for your line, but belts and watches?!

The beaches are full of people sunbathing, playing in the sand, or paddling in the sea, so where are the inflatables, the bat and balls, the sun creams, the bottles of water, the caps and visors, the parasols?

What's missing in this situation? Obviously the sales technique might not be up to scratch, but what's the main reason sales are so poor?

It's all down to a little thing that's missing, called Market Research. I often wonder what the effect on sales would be, had these people asked their potential customers 'what would you like?', and then made that product available the next day. By failing to ask the basic questions, you're always going to be guessing at what your customers really want.

MIRROR MIRROR ON THE WALL

I have often heard the line *"You can always judge the quality of a business through its toilets"*, have you?

If this was really the case then the Alton Towers Hotel and Theme Park in Staffordshire would be the best in the world.

Picture the scene: you're washing your hands with soap and water by the sinks; you shake off the excess water and proceed to dry them under the machine. As you are about to leave the restroom there is a large, full length mirror for you to check your hair etc. Beside the mirror is a plaque that reads "Mirror, mirror on the wall, who's the fairest of them all"; as you stand in front of the mirror a female voice from the gods says "Hey, George Clooney, you've got some competition today. You look hot, baby!"

Laugh? I nearly fell over! Then I created a video all about it (you can see it in action on my YouTube Channel).

In every room of your business there is an opportunity to stand out from the crowd. Take a long hard look at your office, hallways, lifts/ elevators, board rooms, reception areas, and even the car park, and think how you can bring greater interaction to your brand.

MARKETING QUIZ: HOT DOGGING

So how do you create buzz around your brand using social media? Ultimately it's all about creating and encouraging interaction: you've got to be interactive in order to reach out to your followers and friends.

This is great advice, but just how do you create interaction? I dare say there are dozens of ways to achieve this, but one I have personally found, that works time and time again, involves posing simple but creative marketing questions which then take my friends and followers away from their everyday lives.

This is how I do it....

1. First, I set a light-hearted marketing question to test reader's creativity.
2. Next, I mention there is a prize for the most creative answer (remember: an offer is a great way to get a reaction!)
3. A deadline is set for entries.
4. Finally I reveal the Observational Marketing answer, alongside the winner's answer which I have chosen.

The inspiration for these questions comes from the world of Observational Marketing, of course! For example, I was on board a flight to Belfast and was flicking through the in-flight magazine. I came across an article about market stalls in Camden Market, London, and a piece about a hot dog market stand stood out. I quickly took a picture on my phone and uploaded it to Facebook and started the interaction with this light-hearted marketing question:

Q. *"You own a hot dog stand and you want to create a catchy t-shirt, what would it say?"*

I offered copies of both Marketing Takeaway books to the most creative answer and over the weekend I was inundated with some great answers.

I ended up picking 2 winners as I could not decide which was best: *"We serve our dogs with relish"* and *"0% Bark 100% Bite."*

This is Observational Marketing at its best; seeing something that stops you in your tracks and then tweaking it to your business. The T-shirt that I saw in the magazine, on board the plane that day, said *"The Best of The Wurst."*

This form of interaction via social media has seen the greatest amounts of comments, likes and shares with my speaker brand. So what will you do to take your friends and followers away from their normal everyday lives? What prize will tempt them into interacting with you and your brand?

PEEK-A-BOO PROFITS

Every year for the month of December, throngs of people gather and queue, come rain and snow, at a large shop window on Newcastle's Northumberland Street. Parents with travel systems and toddlers jostle alongside teenagers, students and tourists craning to see into the large glass display. The window in question is the full width of the famous Fenwicks department store. Every year during the festive period the window is filled with an elaborate Christmas theme, complete with moving characters and full sound. It's something I always remember watching as a child and it is still going strong today. If you were to ask any Geordie shopper what Fenwicks is famous for they will almost certainly answer the Christmas window!

So let us stay with that theme of excitement and intrigue.

This marketing idea is one that I created for Nicky Gray and Fidgets which is the first hair salon for kids in the North East. The idea is all about creating a buzz on the outside of the salon before children and their parents even step through the door.

We created a world of colour, characters and excitement to fill the windows with eye-catching graphics but within the window graphics are tiny eye-sized holes for children to peep through. When they look inside they see collections of toys, sweets and characters which change every week – a real buggy-stopper and head-turner.

But the intrigue continues inside… children start their hair cut experience by choosing a hair-cut seat/car to sit in, ranging from Brum, to Barbie, to Lightning McQueen. Whilst sitting having their hair cut, they can also watch their self-picked children's DVDs on the plasma screen in front of them. Finally, there is a 'magic tree' where children receive a lollipop after being so well behaved during their hair cut. This all adds up to make a fine, mundane experience into something fab that the young clients can look forward to! Sales and footfall at Fidgets doubled in the first 6 months.

WIN WIN WIN WITH COMPETITIONS

If you want to create interaction, build your database and gain much needed free exposure, create a competition. You will have to give away your products or services, but, believe me, it's worth it.

STEP ONE

Contact the media with an offer to give away your products or services to their readers or listeners.

STEP TWO

Create the competition questions, design the entry form, and send to the media.

STEP THREE

Await coverage.

STEP FOUR

Give the winners their prize and look to convert all entrants into customers by offering samples, vouchers and special offers to everyone who entered.

STEP FIVE

Thank the media with a thoughtful gift!

STEP SIX

Constantly look at additional opportunities during the year to create another competition: Hallowe'en, Easter, Christmas, Summer Holidays, Fathers' & Mothers' Day....

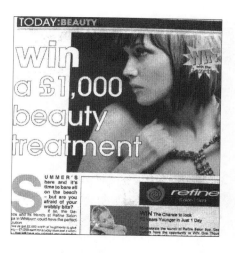

Playing for jersey after kit donation

TWO football teams kicked off the season in style thanks to Bolam Premier Sportswear and the Gazette.

Junior side Hebburn Town Gold FC and senior team Vets Re-United won a full set of strips worth £760.

Ian McDonald, from Vets Re-United, who play in the Sunday Morning Premier League, said: "I received the call from Tricia Bolam and the news did not sink in, so I had to call them back to check that I had actually won.

"I never enter competitions, but I spotted the entry form in Gazette and knew we needed a new set of strips, so I decided to give it a try."

under-eights, who play in the Chase Holmes South Tyneside Youth League, added: "I really like the strip, especially the colours, and I can't wait to play in it."

Shop owner Kevin Bolam said: "We are over the moon to provide a junior and senior team in South Tyneside with a full set of strips.

"We received a lot of entries from clubs, teams and schools in the borough and every team guessed all of the questions correctly, so we put all the entries into a hat, and Hebburn Team Gold and Vets Re-United were chosen.

"The shop is also offering a discount to all the teams that entered the competition off their next

PIC N MIX

A selection of pictures taken throughout my observational travels

A. A great eco reminder from British Airways.

B. Steps leading from an underground car park to a street full of restaurants.

C. A poster situated above a urinal!

D. Chit Chat, even God knows branding.

E. Free jelly worms with every purchase.

F. Great wit and creativity at Ocean Basket, Johannesburg.

G. How Ferrero Rocher promoted christmas at the Metro Centre.

H. Local pub strikes while teachers are on strike.

I. Fantastic postioning as billboard is in front of a building site.

J. How Easy Jet promote their partners on the back of a seat cover.

now that's impressive!

C

With over one million systems fitted so far, TRACKER is UK's leading Stolen Vehicle Recovery system.

TRACKER and the police have been responsible for the recovery of 19,000 stolen vehicles worth a staggering £428million which less

G

FERRERO ROCHER

D

Have a break have a ChitChat with Ben

H

We're not on strike 30 KIDS EAT th FREE June

E

TED BAKER LONDON

I

BEHIND HERE, MEN EARN THEIR BOWTIME

STRONGBOW
HARD EARNED

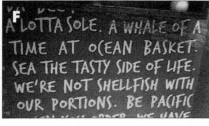

F

A LOTTA SOLE. A WHALE OF A TIME AT OCEAN BASKET. SEA THE TASTY SIDE OF LIFE. WE'RE NOT SHELLFISH WITH OUR PORTIONS. BE PACIFIC

J

Europcar

LOOSEN THAT TIE...
LET US TAKE CARE OF 'FIRST TIME' BUSINESS

easyJet

MARKETING QUIZ:
HEAD TURNER

Q. You own a luxurious online lingerie business and you find out that the Turner Prize is coming to your town. What could you do to get noticed?

A. Following an event I spoke at in Gateshead, Michelle Taylor, from award winning Tallulah Love, was inspired to think of how she could gain exposure without spending any money on advertising.

In a great example of Fusion Marketing, Michelle brought 50 models dressed in her lingerie designs to parade around the Baltic Flour Mill Art Gallery. The models handed out flowers supplied by a local florist, kept warm with a special cocktail from a local bar, wore stickers provided by a local printer, and were picked up by an off-duty double decker bus - with a photographer on hand to capture the whole story for the press.

Social media played a crucial role in bringing together the businesses involved, and was also used to recruit the models. The event coincided with the launch of Tallulah Love's first Viral Marketing video advert, and gained FREE coverage in the regional and national press.

MARKETING QUIZ:
CHOC
THAT

Q. You own a chocolate bar wrapping business. You can custom make any wrapper for any occasion, and you have just become one of 3 finalists to win £50k in the Barclays 'Take One Small Step' competition. The winner is the one who has the most online and text votes. Oh, and Take That are in town! What would you do?

A. I came up with this idea for my client, Laura Kemp, from Choc Cards.

She printed a bar for each member of the band, complete with their image, and details of how to vote for Choc Cards in the competition. We hand-delivered the bars to the stadium in the hope that Gary, Robbie, Mark, Jason and Howard may just eat them and vote…

Now we'll never know if the band did, or not, but we generated amazing publicity through the radio and regional press, based on being a finalist and what we had done for the group.

The result… Laura managed to gain more votes than the other finalists and won the overall prize of £50,000.00 which has taken her business to the next level.
A fantastic outcome generated with such a small financial outlay!

Whatever the occasion, always look for the opportunities around you, and make sure you take advantage to get your business noticed.

Could it be magic for chocolate entrepreneur?

Caren Dent
...
...media.co.uk

SUNDERLAND chocolate entrepreneur is hoping the lake That touch will help her scoop a top small business and £50,000 to invest in growing her business.

... Kemp and her mum Gaye ... Lutt started ChocCards three ... to produce personalised ... bar wrappers for special oc...

... is now shortlisted in the ... Take One Small Step com... and if she receives the most ... June 26, she will win £50,000 ... vest in the firm.

... tried to boost her chances ... delivering personally-de... Robbie Williams, Gary Barlow, ... Jason Orange and Howard ... chocolate bars to the Stadium ... the band's last night at the ... last week.

... said: "I just hope when they ... firm they may even vote for ... Unfortunately I can't see how ... people have voted for me or who ... ted but I am hoping they just ... to win £50,000 would be in... and would do so much for our ...

ique corporate gift

High quality Belgian milk chocolate

Branded with corporate identity and cont

Ideal for promotions, busine

---

te

NT report exposing ... sted on ineffective ... ning courses is "the ..." says a North East

... by the National Au... ...tes the Civil Serv... ...dreds of millions ... year putting staff ... training courses ... Fewer than half of ... felt the training they ... last 12 months had ... their job better ... managing director of ... ased The Test Fac... ... to say that these ... ... me at all, and ... just the tip of the ... culture of poorly-... ...lopment.

... in both the pub... ... for are aware that ... ... out of the staff ... ... them regular per-... ...opportunities but ... ... give far too little ... ...ir staff's individ... ...how best to meet ... ...adopt a sheep-dip ...

...ining needs can ... ...ed learning plans ... ...reas for improve-...

www.chocca

PRIZE WINNERS: Gaye Shakeshaft and Laura Kemp of ChocCards won won the Barclays Take One Small Step competition.

... how gro

GENTO... Customer (CSE) Ac...

The CS ... Governme... ...nising orga... ...onstrate a ... commitme... across all b

The star ... categories ... insight, the cu... sation, inform... delivery and t... ity of service.

The final pa... volved a rigor... assessment.

A Governm... sessor intervie... bers of Gento... and partners ... groups.

Director of ... ence David Di... delighted to be ... high quality of ... that we offer to ...

"At Gentoo ... at the heart o... and this awar... ongoing comm... taining, improv... high levels of ... – further emb... service into the ... ganisation."

Tax-r...
chan
welc

A LEADIN... ...tion has we... changes to t...

Cash prize
is so sweet

SUCCESS ...

£200 MUGG OF COFFEE

Much exposure has been given to the famous Starbucks chain for asking the names of the customers as they take their order, then calling them out once their drink is ready. I personally love the fact they have done this, as to bring a piece of personalisation into proceedings can only be a good thing.

But there is a certain coffee chain that takes this further. Never mind your name; how about remembering your football team, your business, and many other finer points of your life?

I am talking here about the wonderful Mugg & Bean in Gauteng, Johannesburg. I had not been there for around 4 months but as I walked in with my good, friend and fellow speaker, Michael

Jackson, 3 staff members- including the manager, Reggie - came over to shake our hands, asked how we both were and then... asked how my football team, Sunderland, were doing!

I could not believe that they had remembered my team, never mind my name! This barista team are a special blend, THEY REMEMBER - THEY CARE and as a result people like Michael and I go there all the time. In fact, Michael spends over £200 on coffees there each year!

If you can remember the little details, your customers will remember you, and they'll keep on coming back!

WHICH CAME 1ST, THE CHICKEN OR RABBIT?

No matter what size of business or budget you have, you can always find a way to bring engagement, excitement, and attraction to your brand.

Over the Easter Holidays I observed two great marketing ideas whilst on a family holiday in Yorkshire: one from a global brand, and one from a micro business, but which one came out on top, the chicken or the rabbit?

The Rabbit was spotted outside the McArthur Glen Shopping Centre, York. A giant inflatable Lindt Easter bunny created excitement and interest in the brand for shoppers walking by. These blow-up bunnies were spotted all over the globe during the Easter period.

The Chicken was seen at Brambles Antique shop in Thornton le Dale.

The shop owners had placed tiny plastic chickens in the windows, and asked customers to count their chickens before entering the shop with their answer, with a prize for every correct answer!

For me, the Chicken beat the Rabbit. Both captured my attention, but as we entered the shop after Easter Monday the owner told me he had had lots of attention and that it had been great for business. Grace guessed how many chicks there were in the window, and although we were too late to enter, moments later he appeared with a Cadburys chocolate egg for her.

So, are the Easter holidays on your marketing Busy Bee agenda for next year?

SEE WITH RELISH

This is quite possibly one of the greatest examples of marketing and gaining a competitive advantage I have ever seen.

On Christmas Day, 2011, Sanet Gouws walked into a well-known burger chain in Pretoria, South Africa, with her sister and mother. Moments after sitting down with her food she was asked to leave by a member of staff. The reason? Sanet had a dog with her – a guide dog, as Sanet is blind. What followed was a huge PR disaster for this burger chain as the story caused widespread outrage.

But what occurred soon after this is all about gaining an amazing competitive advantage. I spend a lot of time speaking in South Africa, and on a trip to Sun City I met and spoke with Enoch, the manager of Wimpy. He told me that they had created a menu entirely written in braille for their blind customers.

Not only did they create the menu, they also contacted the three braille institutes in Johannesburg with promotional burgers.

The burger buns had each been individually hand-decorated with sesame seeds used to write in braille on the top of the bun. For the very first time blind customers could see what they were going to eat!

What followed next is pure marketing genius. A video was shot and uploaded onto YouTube which has been seen by hundreds of thousands of people all over the world... And very soon you, too! By creating and delivering just 15 braille burgers, news of Wimpy's new all-braille menus was shared with over 800,000 sight disabled people, and thousands of others, too.

So what can we learn from such a campaign?

We need to embrace such creative thinking, and make sure we respond in a great way if a competitor fails to deliver. Congratulations, Wimpy, and, as they say in South Africa, this is lekker!

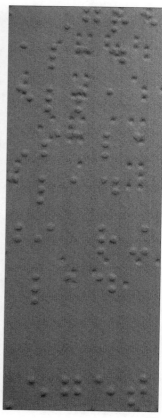

MARKETING QUIZ:
ROCKET FUEL

Q. You run a BP petrol station. Amongst all of the electronic and branded signs, and marketing points of sale, you want to interact with passing motorists and put a smile on their faces. What would you do?

A. Alison Truist owns the BP garage, and every day for the last 40 years Alison and her family have written a funny or motivational message on a large blackboard with chalk.

Her customers love and comment on it, and drivers frequently drive in, fill up, and take the time to say how much they love it.

Marketing expense = pennies; Great Marketing = priceless!

My video blog featuring Alison and one of her famous signs can be viewed on my Great Marketing Ideas YouTube channel.

After seeing my own marketing quotes via social networks, Alison asked if she could feature my messages on her future signs… I'm delighted to say she did just that!

A ROYAL WAVE OF CREATIVITY

When major events take over the regional, national, or international press, you have three main options: you can ignore them, you can watch them, OR, you can decide to join the conversation and use the big event as an opportunity to interact with, and attract, customers.

To celebrate the Queen's Diamond Jubilee in 2012, certain brands chose to join in the festivities and boost their interaction. Some simply donned the national colours to bring the Union Jack Flag to their packaging, instantly making them stand out on the shelves, but what more could you do?

Could you tweak your product? M&Ms created a limited edition pack by changing the colour of their sweets to red, white and blue.

Could you change the name? Kingsmill bread renamed themselves Queensmill, in honour of Her Majesty's 60th year. They also drove sales by offering a free

gift if you bought a few loaves - a fantastic Jubilee tray for your street party sandwiches. Now here is a brand that will be kept in your house for years to come!

OMG do you remember Lydia Leith (www.lydialeith.com) from earlier in the book? Well, here she is again! Not only did she create Jubilee sick bags, but she also launched temporary tattoos and a Queen's head jelly mould! Just like the first time around with her Royal Wedding sick bags, she gained fabulous exposure in the national press and on the BBC, and her Jubilee sick bags were discussed in Fearne Cotton's interview with pop star, Paloma Faith.

So are you ready to interact and attract, or will you sit back and watch or ignore. At some point in the future there will be a new King; perhaps another wedding; maybe even the patter of tiny feet. Red, white and blue... what could you do?

And of course Mainsgill Farm & Tea Room were at it again!!!!

HAPPY BIRTHDAY

Forget sending cards or presents and celebrate your business birthday by doing something big, something different and something memorable!

The release of this book coincides with my 10th year in business, and to celebrate I wanted to do something that will be remembered for years to come.

So what did I do? I saw an opportunity to be creative, and then great marketing happened!

The 'Great Event' took place on the evening of the 2nd April 2012. I brought together some of the greatest speakers and business minds who have inspired me over the years, for a one off event at the Customs House Theatre in South Shields.

I needed some great Sponsor Me Please companies, and SAGE and South Tyneside Council came on board. I used Fusion Marketing to attract over 16 associate sponsors including Free & Easy donations of expertise and products from Purely Mint (SIZE DOES MATTER invites – they were A4 and huge! - mugs & t-shirts), Ian West Photography (PR shots to promote in the media with news releases and social media) Choc Cards (Great Event printed chocolate bar raffle tickets) and Spacecraft who designed and built an incredible stage.

Friends, colleagues and supporters travelled many miles to be at the event, and over 300 businesses packed into the theatre, raising over £10,000 for the Bubble Appeal (Bubble Foundation UK) to help in their fight to save babies born without an immune system.

Marketing is fun, marketing is creative, but most of all, great marketing makes a difference.

Me & Denise Roberston, patron of the Bubble Foundation

Photography by Ian West
(left to right) Michael Jackson, Kevin Morley, Richard McCann, Me & Kevin Gaskell

THE END
FOR NOW!

So there you go, from edible business cards to interactive competitions; from sexy text to becoming a gladiator; from stripping off to ice breakers.

I very much hope you have already taken away some of these Observational Marketing ideas to help you and your business really stand out from the competition, and that you've discovered the Observational Marketeer within.

I still have the ambition to become the next Milk Tray man, and each of the businesses I've mentioned in this book has done something different enough to be remembered. So whether your ambition is to be remembered in 30 days, 30 months, or 30 years, find the opportunities, get creative, and whatever your budget, get out there!

WISHING YOU EVERY MARKETING SUCCESS

To book me as a speaker or to watch more OMG moments...

Email: geoff@geofframm.com
Website: geofframm.com
YouTube: Great Marketing Ideas

SPEND £75*
AND RECEIVE
A LUXURY GIFT
BOX FROM TED

01347 838200

Vote Amelia Lily
4J SKADS EXPRESS

PACHA
INVADES
PACHA
Lineda

Fine Fettle Cycle are now selling

Sledges...!!!

Sliding Pan Sledge £4.99
Toboggan Sledge £14.99
Winter Gloves from £9.9

words were
translated into Farsi at the
event. During his trip to Iran,
also travelled to Isfahan to
speak at the Sustainable
competition in The Market
conference 2009.
Mr Ramm said: "This year has
been my most successful year
speaker with keynote talks
king place all over the UK,
I am already putting in
ace plans to speak in South
rica in 2010, but for now the
to Iran has been the
hlight of an incredible
"

Ye Old Corner Sho

rambles Antiques & Collectables

eaker' in Iran

e Grea

eative

tdoors

Made in the USA
Charleston, SC
05 July 2014